Praise for *Foreign Corrupt Pract*
Resource for Managers an

"Aaron Murphy's book is absolutely fantastic. As a seasoned lawyer and compliance professional, having worked for Fortune 100 companies with global operations for many years and being an FCPA expert myself, I have never come across a more detailed yet easy to read book on FCPA. It contains practical advice and provides examples that are put into context, that the reader can easily relate to and that take into consideration different cultures and customs. A must-read for any individual/organization doing business abroad."

—Fabiana Lacera-Allen, Senior Vice President & Chief Compliance Officer, Elan Drug Technologies

"This book is essential reading for anyone conducting business outside U.S. borders. Executives, managers, sales, marketing, finance, and legal professionals will find sound practical advice to protect themselves and their companies from FCPA violations when operating globally. Much more than a general survey, this book offers scores of real-world examples and serves as an easy-to-read, how-to resource for employees at all levels of a company. It will be a valuable reference tool for many years to come."

—Jeff Taylor, former U.S. Attorney for the District of Columbia and former counselor to Attorneys General John Ashcroft and Alberto Gonzales

"If you are a manager involved in any kind of international dealings— which is to say, if you work for any major firm in today's global marketplace—you need to study Aaron Murphy's comprehensive, precise, and highly readable analysis of life under the Foreign Corrupt Practices Act (FCPA). Few FCPA violations are intentional, yet the consequences even of unwitting violations can be drastic for you, your colleagues, and your firm. Murphy's book shows why business practices perfectly acceptable at home are federal crimes in other settings, how to think your way through ambiguous situations, and—perhaps most important—when to get expert advice. It is a field guide to a world where authority and discretion are all too often up for sale, and a resource that will help you avoid trouble—and even succeed—within the bounds of this crucial yet little-understood legislation."

—Michael Johnston, Charles A. Dana Professor of Political Science, Colgate University

"Every businessperson working in the emerging markets should read and understand the way in which their actions and behaviour may fall subject to the FCPA. This book is a great practical guide to a complex law."

—Scott Lane, Principal and CEO, The Red Flag Group

"Most business managers have heard of the FCPA, but few truly understand the breadth of the FCPA as applied to real-world scenarios. Murphy, an FCPA practitioner with extensive real-world experience, provides an easy-to-read FCPA handbook for business managers. This book is essential reading for business managers looking to develop and implement risk management policies and procedures in this era of aggressive FCPA enforcement."

—Professor Mike Koehler, Butler University, Editor–FCPA Professor Blog

Foreign Corrupt Practices Act

A Practical Resource for Managers and Executives

AARON G. MURPHY

WILEY

John Wiley & Sons, Inc.

Copyright © 2011 by Aaron Gregory Murphy. All rights reserved.

Published by John Wiley & Sons, Inc., Hoboken, New Jersey.

Published simultaneously in Canada.

No part of this publication may be reproduced, stored in a retrieval system, or transmitted in any form or by any means, electronic, mechanical, photocopying, recording, scanning, or otherwise, except as permitted under Section 107 or 108 of the 1976 United States Copyright Act, without either the prior written permission of the Publisher, or authorization through payment of the appropriate per-copy fee to the Copyright Clearance Center, Inc., 222 Rosewood Drive, Danvers, MA 01923, (978) 750-8400, fax (978) 646-8600, or on the Web at www.copyright.com. Requests to the Publisher for permission should be addressed to the Permissions Department, John Wiley & Sons, Inc., 111 River Street, Hoboken, NJ 07030, (201) 748-6011, fax (201) 748-6008, or online at http://www.wiley.com/go/permissions.

Limit of Liability/Disclaimer of Warranty: While the publisher and author have used their best efforts in preparing this book, they make no representations or warranties with respect to the accuracy or completeness of the contents of this book and specifically disclaim any implied warranties of merchantability or fitness for a particular purpose. No warranty may be created or extended by sales representatives or written sales materials. The advice and strategies contained herein may not be suitable for your situation. You should consult with a professional where appropriate. Neither the publisher nor author shall be liable for any loss of profit or any other commercial damages, including but not limited to special, incidental, consequential, or other damages.

For general information on our other products and services or for technical support, please contact our Customer Care Department within the United States at (800) 762-2974, outside the United States at (317) 572-3993 or fax (317) 572-4002.

Wiley also publishes its books in a variety of electronic formats. Some content that appears in print may not be available in electronic formats. For more information about Wiley products, visit our Web site at www.wiley.com.

Library of Congress Cataloging-in-Publication Data:

Murphy, Aaron G.
    Foreign corrupt practices act : a practical resource for managers and executives/ Aaron G. Murphy.
        p. cm.
    Includes index.
    ISBN 978-0-470-91800-5 (pbk.); ISBN 978-0-470-93962-8 (ebk);
ISBN 978-0-470-93963-5 (ebk); ISBN 978-0-470-94865-1 (ebk)
    1. Business ethics—United States. 2. Management—Moral and ethical aspects—United States. 3. Bribery—United States. 4. Corporations—United States—Corrupt practices. 5. United States. Foreign Corrupt Practices Act of 1977. I. Title.
    HF5387.M8757 2011
    658.1'20973—dc22

                                                                    2010032316

Printed in the United States of America.

10 9 8 7 6 5 4 3 2 1

For Jennifer, Max, and Viv.
This book represents many hours
away from home.
I intend to make it up to each of you.

Disclaimer

This book does not provide legal advice, nor does it create an attorney–client relationship between the author or the author's firm and anyone owning, possessing, or reading this book. The examples used in this book either come from published cases or are based on amalgamations from the author's own experience, modified for illustrative purposes. Any similarities between examples used herein and any actual events are purely coincidental. Because the resolution of legal questions is always fact-specific, always consult your own legal counsel about your particular situation.

Contents

Foreword

A aron Murphy has written a marvelous book on the increasingly complex and difficult challenges posed by the Foreign Corrupt Practices Act (FCPA). The FCPA, enacted in 1977, was a revolutionary statute that outlawed corrupt payments to foreign government officials at a time when such bribery was all too common and, indeed, not prohibited (and indeed in many cases facilitated by tax laws) in the home countries of many corporations, like Germany and Japan.

Over time, that landscape has slowly changed. Many governments, notably in the OECD, have enacted laws forbidding bribery. And just as importantly, some governments have significantly increased their enforcement efforts. For example, prosecutors in Germany led the way in pursuing the landmark case against Siemens, something that would have been unthinkable ten years earlier. Just this year, the United Kingdom enacted a new and broader anti-corruption law that it has promised to vigorously enforce. Both strong laws and vigorous enforcement are critical to ensuring continued progress against improper payments.

As Aaron vividly describes, the United States—through both the Department of Justice and the Securities and Exchange Commission—has led the way in ramping up its enforcement efforts. The number of recent FCPA prosecutions and the penalties imposed (including lengthy prison sentences for company executives) eclipse the figures seen in previous decades. This is one of many good reasons to read Aaron's excellent book.

The FCPA is at one level deceptively simple, prohibiting corrupt payments to non-U.S. government officials and requiring accurate books and records and a system of sufficient internal controls. But that simplicity masks a host of complex issues—as does the increasingly aggressive enforcement of the FCPA. This is particularly so with the books and records and controls provisions of the FCPA. The resulting dilemmas, as Aaron discusses, can involve everything from mooncakes to charitable contributions to a bribe demand at 1 A.M. on a lonely highway in a faraway place. Aaron leads the reader through the thicket of issues raised by the FCPA and its enforcement in a practical and lively way—with more than a sprinkle of provocative (and, I might say, justified) controversy over some of the enforcement actions (or rather, settlements) Aaron discusses.

What I love most about Aaron's book, however, is its emphasis on culture, leadership, and process in addressing FCPA risk. As Aaron puts it, "it is poor recordkeeping and lack of procedures and controls that get most people in trouble." Put succinctly, "[t]he single best way [to keep your company out of trouble] is to ensure that your company has the best compliance program possible." That requires a focus on prevention, detection of potential issues and strong response—for no company is perfect and none is composed of 100 percent perfect employees, much less perfect agents, distributors, and other third parties. To translate these strategies into practice, companies must establish a forceful tone at the top (and in the middle), strong processes and procedures around FCPA (and other) risks, good mechanisms to detect issues (like an ombuds program), and no-nonsense response when an issue arises.

The FCPA has been a tremendous force for fair competition and the rule of law in the thirty-three years of its life. But it is not an easy law to understand or to keep abreast of in all its complexity. Aaron's book is an ideal and interesting walk through that landscape. It will be helpful to specialists, and even more so to business leaders and managers in doing what the overwhelming majority of those leaders and managers strive to do—lead with integrity.

Brackett Denniston
Senior Vice President and General Counsel
General Electric Company
August 2010

Acknowledgments

Writing a book is a lonely affair, but I have the very good fortune of being married to Jennifer Gully, a wonderful woman who is not merely supportive but also a talented lawyer and author in her own right. Without her insights, critical eye, and willingness to put up with my interminable talk about this project, I would never have finished it, and it wouldn't have been any good even if I had.

I also have to thank my colleagues David Schindler, Doug Greenburg, and Dan Seltzer for their thoughts and comments, both on this book and in general over the many thousands of hours we have worked together. In addition, my friends at Ernst & Young who reviewed the manuscript and offered critiques and insight also warrant mention here, particularly Amanda Massucci, Jonathan Feig, Richard Sibery, Brian Loughman, Chris Richardson, and Jeff Taylor.

And finally, this would not be a book at all were it not for Tim Burgard at John Wiley & Sons. His enthusiasm for this project meant the difference between a manuscript that sits in a desk drawer and the book in your hand. I could not have asked for better luck than I had when this project founds its way to his desk.

Introduction

Who Is This Book For?

This book is for managers.

Primarily, it is for managers in U.S. companies or companies listed on a U.S. stock exchange. And if you are a U.S. citizen (or national, or lawful permanent resident) working abroad, even for a non-U.S. company, this book is for you, too.

In either case, you are subject to the Foreign Corrupt Practices Act—more commonly called the FCPA. The FCPA is the United States' foreign anti-bribery law and, regardless of whether you work in a sales, marketing, business development, operations, or financial capacity, it governs your conduct anywhere in the world, any time.

Even if you are not on the ground in a foreign country right now, odds are that you will be one day or at least will be involved with foreign aspects of a company's business during the course of your career. Globalization being what it is, most U.S. businesses of any significant size have, or soon will have, operations abroad. In all such cases, FCPA compliance is mandatory.

I handle FCPA matters all around the world, and over the years I've seen the same scenario time and time again: Despite the existence of a corporate compliance program, despite having sat through a PowerPoint presentation about the basic elements of the FCPA, despite the best intentions of everyone, many managers still do not see real live FCPA problems until it's too late (if they see them at all). Later, when the internal or external auditors find them, or a call registers on the company's whistle-blower hotline, or an in-house attorney is asked to consult on a transaction and learns about some suspicious activities that have already occurred, a lot of hard questions are asked and careers can be damaged or ruined. The goal of this book is to stop that from happening.

In my experience, almost no manager—whether young and looking ahead to a long and successful career, or very senior and looking ahead to a long and relaxing retirement—ever actually intends to violate the FCPA. (I've seen intentional violations, but they are rare.) Far more common is that a lower-level employee intends to get ahead (by boosting sales, landing a big account, or simply playing big shot by hobnobbing with important government officials) and the manager fails to catch it. When the post mortem is done months or even years later, by lawyers and forensic accountants, the red flags and warning signs seem to be everywhere. I've had many discussions with in-house lawyers and audit committee members where, when the facts are laid out, they all shake their heads and say, "What were they thinking? How could our managers have missed this?"

You don't want to be one of those managers.

As you might imagine, it's often the lower-level managers who get in the most trouble because they are the ones closest to the problem. In what may be the cruelest irony of all, those with the least experience doing business abroad are often the ones expected to spot all of the potential problems and raise questions to the appropriate people (their supervisors, the in-house legal department, compliance officer, etc.), and to do so while they are trying to get their hands around a new assignment in a new and often disorienting country and business culture.

This book is not intended to be an exhaustive course on the FCPA. As a manager, you have a business to run. If you wanted to become an expert in a highly nuanced legal specialty, you'd have gone to law school. Instead, this book is intended to be a discussion of what I see as the most common problem areas where managers get themselves into FCPA trouble. The impetus for this book was my conclusion that, although many companies have compliance and training programs, most materials that I have reviewed do not have examples from the real world. Managers walk out of trainings with a sense that it is all academic and that bribery could never happen on their watch. But bribery does happen, all the time.

Much of the education managers receive about the FCPA does not give them any sense of how violations often occur. Everyone understands that they can't trade money for a government contract, but very few understand that donating money to a perfectly legitimate charity that happens to be a pet project of a government official may also violate the FCPA. Or worse, that the supposedly fancy mooncakes you approved as Chinese New Year gifts might not be mooncakes at all, but gift certificates that are fully redeemable for cash.

I use these and many other examples from real cases that I have either seen myself or that are part of the FCPA literature, and I try to boil it all down into something that you can actually use in your day-to-day life.

To write this book, I asked myself what I would tell a mid-level manager about the FCPA during a two-hour dinner. My hope is that you have already seen the movies available on your twentieth flight to Hong Kong, Singapore, Dubai, or wherever it is you're headed next, and will find this book in your bag, crack it open, and be better prepared to deal with FCPA issues when you land than when you left.

And you'll know what you can and cannot do when that customs agent looks down at your passport, shakes his head, rubs his thumb and index finger together, and says with a grin: "This could take awhile."

CHAPTER 1

Basics of the Foreign Corrupt Practices Act

In its most basic formulation, the Foreign Corrupt Practices Act (FCPA) prohibits bribery of foreign government officials. But, as with most things legal, it is far more complex than that.

The notion of foreign bribery conjures up an image of a briefcase full of cash being handed off at the edge of a dusty airstrip in some vaguely tropical locale, or handing over a passport with a folded sheaf of bills tucked inside to an armed member of a militia or police organization that may or may not have any real authority. In truth, the vast majority of foreign bribes are far more mundane (although I once was held at gunpoint in Indonesia, resulting in a payment that will be discussed in Chapter 9).

Under the FCPA, a "bribe" is the offer or promise of anything of value, made to a foreign official, with the intent to obtain or retain business or to secure an unfair business advantage. As you will see, that sentence is far more complex than you might imagine. We'll go over all of these concepts in great detail in this book, but at the outset let's focus on the idea of obtaining or retaining business or securing an advantage. When you think about it, virtually everything you do in your business life is intended to obtain or retain business or an advantage of some kind. Everything. The implications of this can be startling.

What this means is that FCPA violations often involve actions that, in a private commercial context, are not only permissible but commonplace. You take your best customer out for an expensive dinner, complete with a nice bottle of wine and port for dessert, just to hammer out the final details of a new contract. You fly potential customers to a resort for a company conference to talk about your latest products and, between rounds of golf and spa treatments, you try to convince them that your product is better than your competitor's. You give a donation to the favorite charity of the CEO of a huge potential customer, just to build a relationship that may bear fruit in the future. You remember to send customers cases of wine during the holidays, anniversary presents, tokens of congratulations upon the graduation or wedding of their children. Use of the company's skybox during the playoffs. Concert tickets. The list goes on and on. The only reason you do any of these things is to obtain or retain business.

All of these things, done in the normal course of business with regular customers, can be crimes if done with foreign government officials under the right conditions. They are not always FCPA violations, but they certainly could be, depending on the circumstances. The point of this book is not to conclusively resolve whether specific examples are violations—leave that analysis (and the liability for getting it wrong) to your legal or corporate compliance departments. The point of this book is to ensure that you see the potential problems before it is too late and get the help you need.

"Anything of Value" Can Be Considered a Bribe

Under the FCPA, you cannot give foreign government officials "anything of value" if you intend to influence them in connection with obtaining or retaining business. If you do, it might be a bribe under the FCPA.

A bribe can take many forms. Cash is obvious, concert tickets less obvious, a meal that's perhaps a little too nice even less obvious, and a slightly excessive salary to an employee who is the spouse of a government official who might help your business crosses the line in a way that very few managers would spot.

Beyond these kinds of direct payments and gifts, there is the whole universe of payments made by third-party consultants and advisors. Ask yourself if you really know where all the money went that you paid the consultant who helped you get the permits and business licenses you needed for your new factory; or the local tax advisor who managed to straighten out the issue you had with the local authorities; or your freight forwarder and customs agent who told you about a special permit that would miraculously allow your goods to clear customs within a day of arrival (or without being subject to the normal, time-consuming inspections).

Think about every line item on every invoice from every third-party service provider, every expense approved for reimbursement to your sales team, and every use of petty cash, and ask yourself if you really understand what those charges and expenses were and where the money went. Do that and you will have a sense of the endless places FCPA violations can hide.

Worse yet, imagine what you would say to someone like me—a very cynical lawyer—who questioned you, two, three, or five years later, about a certain line item on a certain invoice that you (or your staff) approved. I have had a hundred of these conversations, and they are all pretty much the same: The description on the invoice is vague and the amount fairly large, the managers do not remember anything about it, although they plainly see their initials or signature on the approval line. Yes, they attended an FCPA training, but it never occurred to them that this could be a problem. They trusted their people. "Hey, I rely on my finance guy to check this stuff." But the audit committee always has the same reaction: "Why didn't they catch this? It's obvious."

The problem is that the FCPA is all-inclusive. The actual text of the statute uses the phrase "anything of value," and it truly means *anything*. Any economic benefit of any kind whatsoever whether paid directly or through an agent on the company's behalf. Anything. Any amount, no matter how small.

In the United States, many government agencies have strict ethics rules that forbid their employees from receiving even the most minimal gifts. In fact, when I have met with lawyers from the Securities and Exchange Commission (SEC) at my office, I generally schedule the meetings so they do not overlap with lunch. The reason is to avoid the uncomfortable situation where the SEC lawyers try to pay for the sandwiches that are often ordered for lunch meetings. The SEC has strict rules prohibiting its staff from accepting almost anything. The sandwiches are obviously of trivial value, and I would never think for a second that the SEC would have mercy on my client because we gave them a turkey sandwich (were it only that easy!), but they decline them nonetheless.

I tell you this only because I find that many managers simply cannot believe that providing something as small as a meal or a few cocktails could possibly constitute a federal crime. But if the SEC honestly believes that a mediocre conference room sandwich worth, at most, a couple of dollars might compromise the ethics of its own agents, you'd better believe it will take the view that a steak dinner at the Four Seasons in Hong Kong or a spot of 25-year Macallan could compromise the integrity of a Chinese government employee who makes only a few hundred dollars per month.

I often hear clients tell me that a particular expense was "reasonable" or "modest," or that it was not "unreasonable," as if such a determination resolves the question of whether the FCPA has been violated. I am not sure how those concepts made their way into so many heads, but they gloss over the realities of the FCPA. Anything means anything. The statute's focus is not on the value of the gift but the intent of the giver.

The Corrupt Motive Problem: Don't Assume—Run It Up the Chain

To violate the FCPA, offers or gifts of anything of value must be made "corruptly." This "corrupt motive" requirement—generally understood to mean a payment made with the intent to influence the government official in some way—should not cause too much heartburn. When an issue arises, a prudent manager should raise it to the appropriate personnel and let them deal with the difficult questions surrounding corrupt motive. As I discuss later on in Chapter 10 about books and records, this is rarely a stumbling block for the government, and it shouldn't be for a manager either.

When clients use a term like "reasonable" or "unreasonable" to describe the size of a gift or payment, they use it as a proxy for a much more complex set of concepts: knowledge and intent. If the value is small, they seem to be saying, it couldn't possibly be intended as a bribe. That *may* be true (certainly the low value of the gift or payment could be *evidence* of lack of corrupt intent on the part of the giver), but it is not conclusive.

As discussed, giving a sandwich to an SEC lawyer is extremely unlikely to be seen as a bribe by any reasonable person, but the SEC's flat prohibition on such "gifts" is designed to avoid any difficult questions asked after the fact. That is really how a manager should think about the concepts of knowledge and intent. Avoid the appearance of impropriety. If something looks bad, it is assumed to be bad, and explaining it away after the fact can be extremely challenging.

Although the FCPA requires the "corrupt motive" to exist in the mind of the giver, the more important notion of corruption is often in the mind of the beholder. What would the company's compliance officer, general counsel, or audit committee members think the gift or payment was for? How would the company's outside counsel view it? How would the Department of Justice (DOJ) view it?

Viewing even innocuous transactions through hindsight complicates the analysis because these issues do not arise in isolation. Small payments, gifts, meals, and the like tend to occur in clusters or patterns. When resolving a regulatory issue, making a large sale, or getting the necessary licenses, certifications, or permitting issues resolved, there is generally a series of meetings. When those meetings include meals, entertainment, or small gifts, and the end result is favorable to the company, the entire series of transactions can look suspicious. While it is true that the U.S. government is unlikely to bring a criminal case over a single steak dinner, there is rarely a single instance.

The fundamental question for FCPA purposes—whether these gifts, meals, and so on—were made with a corrupt motive becomes a nearly impossible question to resolve. Of course the employees in question will always say they never intended to influence anyone. Yet, when asked why the meeting took place in a nice restaurant instead of a conference room at the office, they will just as often say that they need to "maintain a good relationship" with the government officials in question. So what exactly was the motive, and was some or all of it corrupt? Hard to say.

As the value of what is given increases, the question generally gets easier to resolve. Having the business meeting on the company yacht over a long weekend is more problematic than drinks at a club. Flying the official and his family to the United States to attend the meeting and then footing the bill for them all to take a weeklong vacation is even more problematic. But even relatively small amounts pose thorny questions that can be time consuming and expensive to address once they come under the microscope.

Detailed examples of these gift and entertainment problems are discussed in their own chapters later in this book. But for now, the basic message is this: Don't be fooled by small amounts. There is no exception for "reasonable" expenses, and you often won't be able to see the larger pattern of gifts and expenses that may exist because those generally only come out after the lawyers or accountants start digging through your books.

Be cynical and assume a corrupt motive unless you have a compelling reason not to. Don't assume the responsibility for deciding that a small transaction is fine. Transactions always look worse later when the context is lost and all that remains is the cryptic language on a receipt and a reimbursement form. There are people in your company whose job it is to make these judgment calls. Let them do it.

Foreign Officials and Discretionary Authority

The FCPA outlaws payments to foreign officials that are intended to get them to do (or not do) some official act that is within their discretion.

Acts that are not within their discretion (like stamping your passport at the airport when there is no legitimate reason not to) are the kind that may be "facilitated" by a payment, which leads to the much-overused and little-understood FCPA exception for "facilitating" payments. Facilitating payments are discussed in detail in Chapter 9, but the bottom line is that extremely few payments are actually facilitating payments, and no manager should make that call on his or her own.

The FCPA is further complicated by the fact that it defines foreign official in the broadest possible terms, such that it can be difficult to figure out who counts as one. Specifically, the FCPA defines "foreign official" as any employee of a foreign government "or instrumentality thereof." This extremely broad language brings employees at what are commonly called state-owned enterprises under the reach of the law. Thus, the purchasing manager at a state-owned shipping company in China would be a foreign official under the FCPA. So would a doctor at a state-owned hospital in Poland.

To make matters worse, the state-owned entity need not be fully owned by the foreign government. Indeed, I have heard DOJ prosecutors say that it is not official ownership that they care about but rather the degree of control exerted by the government over the entity in question. Thus, a fully privatized entity in the Kazakhstan oil industry that *used* to be a government entity could still be a state-owned entity for FCPA purposes. This is especially true if the government still appoints the board or effectively runs the company even though it is technically owned by a private citizen (often a retired or former government official who still has close ties to the government). These are difficult, if not outright impossibie, relationships to uncover. The incestuous and often extremely opaque nature of commerce in many foreign countries means that a U.S. business can never really be certain about the nature of its customers, consultants, or business partners in certain parts of the world.

The payments to this very broad and ill-defined group that are prohibited are those intended to get the officials to exercise authority in your favor. That is, to do or refrain from doing, something that is within their discretion as part of their official capacity. This is a slippery definition because, in truth, very little that a foreign official does falls *outside* of this definition. As the next examples show, there are relatively few things a foreign official does that are fully and clearly nondiscretionary in nature.

Consider this: A foreign official in charge of awarding a contract for a major new public works project issues a request for proposals that are not subject to a public bid process. During the bid period, he calls you into his office and informs you that if you will agree to refund 5 percent of the contract price to him, he can guarantee that you will be awarded the contract. You agree and, sure enough, you are awarded the contract.

This is an obvious example of a prohibited transaction. The decision to award the contract rests solely within the discretion of the official, and the official has asked for a direct quid pro quo. You give him 5 percent; he gives you the contract. Enough said.

But what about this: You plan a business trip to Indonesia to negotiate a new contract with your distributor there. You request and receive a proper business visa from the Indonesian consulate in the United States. Yet, when you arrive at the airport in Jakarta, the customs officer inspects your passport, looks you over, spends a several minutes at the computer, asks you a few questions about the purpose of your visit, and generally seems to drag out the process. Finally, she tells you there are some issues with your papers that must be resolved before you can enter the country, and she takes you to a small room. Once inside, she tells you that the official who can resolve the issues is not there, and that you might have a long wait. Perhaps you ask if there is anyone else who can resolve it. Perhaps you just sit a little while. But eventually she tells you that she may be able to expedite things for $20.

Variations on this one are common. Here you have a low-level official who is simply refusing to do her job in the hope of shaking you down. You have a properly issued visa from the Indonesian government obtained before you left the United States. You know it and she knows it. Her job is merely to ensure that everyone entering the country has proper paperwork; if they do, she is supposed to stamp their passports and let them in. She has no discretionary authority to determine whether to stamp a properly presented passport containing a proper visa.

Under this scenario, if you pay her the $20, it is not considered a bribe under the FCPA.

There is a big gap between these two examples, but almost every example that falls into that gap is a potential FCPA violation because it contains some element of discretion on the part of the foreign official.

Try this common problem: A key piece of equipment is broken in your factory in India, effectively shutting down production. The equipment is large and heavy and expensive to ship, but the cost of a two-week shutdown outweighs the cost of air freight, so you pay an outrageous sum to have new equipment flown overnight to Bangalore.

In the rush to get the equipment there right away, certain customs paperwork was not properly filled out and filed. When the equipment arrives at the airport, you are told it will take two weeks to clear customs while the paperwork is properly routed through the various offices and the necessary inspections are performed. You rant and rave to the customs officer, who then takes you aside and tells you that there is a way to expedite clearance, but it's expensive. He tells you that a special permit, or "intervention," "evacuation," or some other official sounding thing can be arranged. "It's common in these situations," he tells you. "It ensures you same-day processing." You ask him about the paperwork that you were told would take two weeks to straighten out. "This is different paperwork," he says. "So that doesn't matter anymore." He names a price. It's absurd, but you decide to pay it. After all, you're already in for the shipping costs, and you don't want the downtime too. The customs officer then refers you to a customs broker who, he says, specializes in these transactions. The broker, of course, is very nearby. Magically, your equipment is through customs in an hour, you have paid the broker, and you return to your office with your new equipment and a receipt for the broker's services that gets filed away somewhere in your accounting department.

Problem? Probably.

I frequently see issues like this. The most common refrain in defense of the payment is that it was purely to facilitate processing. That is, it was merely a payment to skip to the front of the line and nothing more. Setting aside the question of whether skipping to the front of the line is a permissible payment (it can be, but that is a question for Chapter 9), that's not really an accurate description of what happened. Under this scenario, you had equipment that was subject to certain paperwork and inspection requirements. Sure you were skipping to the front of the line, but you were also skipping the paperwork and inspection. The U.S. government may view that as a payment to secure an improper exercise of the customs officer's discretionary authority.

The lesson, then, is that only the most ministerial of acts can possibly fall into the "nondiscretionary" category and hence be truly outside of the FCPA.

You Don't Need to Make the Payment—A Mere Offer or Promise Is Good Enough

Let's go back to the first hypothetical above and change it slightly. Let's say the government official asks for a 5 percent kickback in exchange for awarding your company the contract. You agree, and yet, when the contract is formally awarded sometime later, one of your competitors is given the business.

The common response to questions about these arrangements is that the company never made any payments and never received any business. No harm, no foul, no FCPA violation. But that is wrong. This is still a violation because the FCPA makes it a crime to merely offer a payment.

In fact, we can change the hypothetical even more. Let's say that the 5 percent kickback proposal was your idea (or, more likely, the idea of one of your new, aggressive salespeople). If, in the course of the negotiations, the salesperson tells the official how committed your company is to the official's country and building a strong relationship with the local community and, as part of that, your company would like to make arrangements to refund 5 percent of the contract price back to the community, perhaps through the official himself to distribute however he sees fit. And, at the mere mention of such thing, the official blanches and tells the salesperson to leave immediately. This is still a violation. Just making the offer is a crime.

This is one area that makes a manager's oversight so difficult. Even if the company has the best policies and procedures in place such that they will stop an improper payment from being made, by the time the payment is stopped, the FCPA violation has already occurred. This is why training is so essential to any FCPA compliance program. You want to keep the offers from being made or agreed to when proposed. You want to stop the violations before they happen.

It Doesn't Matter if the Bribe Works: The Focus Is on the Intent of the Giver, Not the Effect on the Recipient

This is merely a twist on the prior discussion, but the point is worth making on its own. The offer does not need to yield any actual business or other improper benefit or advantage to the company. If the offeror *intends* the offer to yield business or an improper advantage, that is all that matters. To circle back to where we began, if the offer is made with the requisite *corrupt motive*, it does not matter in the least if the offer is accepted or if any benefit is actually derived.

This distinction sets up a whole collection of difficult questions because it is quite possible to make an offer of something of value but without any intent that it induce any official to do anything. One common area where this distinction matters is with travel, entertainment, and meals. As discussed, you cannot give an SEC enforcement attorney a sandwich because of this very problem.

We will discuss the issue in more detail in the chapters on travel (Chapter 6), entertainment (Chapter 5), and gifts (Chapter 7), but for now, remember that even failed efforts can be violations. Even total miscommunications can be violations. Imagine the oblivious official—perhaps so used to being lavishly wined and dined that he views your largess as an entitlement, clearly nothing that would warrant special treatment—who accepts your hospitality without even recognizing the clear intent of your marketing people to influence him. It does not matter. If your marketing people have a corrupt motive, this is still a violation.

The FCPA Applies to All U.S. Citizens—Anytime, Anywhere

The ability of a nation to regulate it citizens regardless of whether they are physically within its borders is a very old and well-established rule of international law. There are limits to this power (e.g., a nation cannot require its citizens to do something in another country that is illegal in that country), but these limits are of little practical concern for the average law-abiding citizen. At the end of the day, it really is a crime for a U.S. citizen to buy and smoke a Cuban cigar when he's in Hong Kong, even though they are perfectly legal there. U.S. companies and their employees are bound by many U.S. laws even when they are not in the United States.

That you are subject to the FCPA anywhere in the world is especially important to keep in mind if you are a U.S. citizen, national, or lawful permanent resident who has taken a job abroad for a privately held foreign company. You are still subject to the FCPA even if your employer is not.

The FCPA Requires Accurate Record Keeping and Strong Internal Controls

The FCPA's "books and records" and "internal accounting controls" provisions are perhaps the broadest, most far-reaching, and most dangerous of all U.S. securities laws. The fact of the matter is that these provisions apply to *all* books and records and *all* internal controls—not just those dealing with bribery. Thus, a company with poor books and records can be held in violation of the FCPA even when there are no allegations of foreign bribery, and regardless of whether it does any business overseas at all.

These provisions require companies to "make and keep books, records, and accounts, which, in reasonable detail, accurately and fairly reflect the transactions and dispositions of the assets." The statute goes on to specify that "reasonable detail" means "such level of detail and degree of assurance as would satisfy prudent officials in the conduct of their own affairs." Thus, if you would be more careful with and keep better records of your own assets, you may be running afoul of the record keeping and internal controls provisions of the FCPA.

The FCPA requires companies to keep accurate accounting records to prevent the concealment of bribes. That is, the books and records should clearly state what the company's assets are, and one should easily be able to figure out where and how a company spent its money.

This is easier said than done. It should go without saying that the creation of a completely false invoice used to mask the true nature of an expense (i.e., using an invoice for office supplies to support what was really a withdrawal from petty cash used to pay off a tax inspector) is a books and records violation. Yet difficult questions frequently arise in connection with much more mundane, and possibly innocent, books and records problems.

For example, expenses for any large organization have to be rolled up under broad descriptive categories for accounting purposes simply because there would be no other meaningful way to assess the organization's expenditures. My experience is that most finance or accounting people recognize that, at the margins, certain expenses theoretically could be categorized in a number of ways and that fine distinctions between these categorizations do not matter all that much. Thus, whether a gift to a potential customer is booked as a "promotional expense," a "marketing expense," or as "business development" makes no meaningful difference. On a macro level, the accounting will be accurate enough if any of the three categories are used.

But let's return to the hypothetical with the Indian customs broker from above. After you have paid the customs broker, who miraculously shepherded your equipment through customs in an hour, when you were told it would take two weeks, you return to your office with an invoice from the broker. Not surprisingly, the invoice states that it is for customs brokerage services and contains some form of cryptic description like "customs interference" or "express clearance." You send the invoice to the accounting department, where it is recorded wherever customs-related expenses are normally booked.

The U.S. government would likely take the position that this is a books and records violation under the FCPA, even though the invoice says it is for customs brokerage, and even though it is recorded that way. The government would likely say that the underlying transaction was a bribe (for the same reasons discussed earlier) and, as a result, the description in the books and records is inaccurate. The proper description would be "bribe," not "customs expense."

Most managers laugh at the idea of openly recording something as a bribe, but that is exactly the position the government takes. But because almost no company ever does so, nearly every violation of the FCPA's anti-bribery provisions also results in a corresponding violation of the books and records provisions. As discussed in Chapter 2 on fines and penalties, this becomes significant both for purposes of calculating fines and for creating a means to resolve FCPA cases in a noncriminal manner.

Companies must also maintain appropriate internal controls that allow for the preparation of accurate financial statements and ensure the proper use of corporate assets. Generally, books and records and internal controls problems go hand in hand. Where one is found, the other is usually nearby. I often think of internal controls as a set of policies and procedures designed to keep the fox from guarding the henhouse.

There is no one set of comprehensive internal controls that will fit all companies in all situations. Best practice guidelines are widely available, and every company needs to consult them and implement a set of internal controls that makes sense for its organization. These should include, at minimum, procedures for entering into contracts, hiring agents or consultants, conducting due diligence on potential acquisitions and joint venture partners; policies governing employee reimbursements; policies for gifts, meals, travel, and entertainment; policies relating to marketing and promotional expenses; policies and procedures governing the use of cash and access to cash; structural separation within the organization ensuring that reimbursements and cash requests are overseen by individuals or departments that do not report to the individuals making the requests; in certain countries, such as China, ensuring that access to the company chop—which is necessary for entering into formal contracts—is restricted to appropriate personnel; as well as many other more nuanced policies, procedures, and controls.

"Defenses" That Don't Work

There are a number of common "defenses" I hear in the course of investigating FCPA allegations. These are not really defenses so much as a common set of complaints or outrages shared by a large number of managers and executives when they learn that some relatively common activity in one of their foreign business units might violate the FCPA. I address some of them here just to get them out of the way before we move on to chapters on specific types of activity that can get you into trouble.

"Everyone else does it. What are we supposed to do—just shut down our business?"

The simple answer may be: "Yes." I hear complaints along these lines all the time. There is a reformulated version of this complaint that I actually like as a defense, at least on a theoretical level. The reformulated version goes something like this: "Every competitor pays bribes just to be able to bid or have a fair shot at getting business. And if everyone pays, how is it that I am getting an 'unfair advantage' as required by the FCPA?" Said another way, "I'm not getting an advantage; I'm just leveling the playing field. Keeping up with the Joneses." Clever perhaps, but probably too cute by half. This "defense" is undercut by the old counterargument that "two wrongs don't make a right."

Indeed, one of the leading FCPA cases states: "The fact that other companies were guilty of similar bribery ... does not excuse [the company's] actions; multiple violations of a law do not make those violations legal or create vagueness in the law."

The whole purpose of the FCPA is to fight international corruption. Using the fact of systemic corruption as a basis to excuse compliance with the FCPA turns the law on its head. The fact of the matter is, bribery remains illegal under the local laws of even the most corrupt nations. Thus, the presumed competitor that one is hypothetically gaining an "unfair advantage" over is the *law-abiding* competitor. Thus, the "everyone else does it" excuse will always fall on deaf ears with the U.S. Government. The FCPA does not account for the very real possibility that a law-abiding competitor may in fact be only hypothetical and impossible to find in certain parts of the real world.

"But we've always done it that way. I assumed someone must have signed off on it."

This is the excuse generally offered by the new manager who arrives overseas to find a system already in place. When the system (for bidding, for getting approvals, or for whatever else) turns out to be an FCPA problem, the manager simply says she was just following the protocol already set up when she got there. But failing to cast a critical eye on processes and procedures that predate you generally will not keep you out of trouble.

Under this scenario, the best a manager can hope for is that she will be seen as negligent or ignorant of the business and the law in such a way as to excuse her from personal responsibility. But being viewed this way—that is, as a negligent manager—generally does not do a lot for a manager's long-term career prospects. Worst-case scenario is that the manager's excuse will fall on deaf ears and be viewed by her bosses, the company's board or audit committee, or, worst of all, the government as what is known as "willful blindness."

Willful blindness is the careful—essentially intentional— avoidance of information that would confirm what you suspected was the case all along. Whenever you hear someone say something like "Sure, XYZ country is corrupt. People must pay bribes all the time. But I never saw it. No one ever told me. I didn't know about it and I didn't want to know about it," you are getting awfully close to willful blindness.

Willful blindness is equated with intent for FCPA purposes. Maintaining plausible deniability by refusing to "learn" the last fact or two that would confirm that an illegal act is occurring will not insulate you from liability. This behavior is treated as knowledge in an FCPA prosecution. Bottom line: Be critical, even of processes and procedures that predate you.

"The [foreign] government knew what was going on and approved it. How can that be a violation of U.S. law?"

This is a loose corollary to actions that are actually permitted by the FCPA. The FCPA allows any act permitted under the written laws of the country where the act occurs. As discussed much later in Chapter 9, this defense is of almost no real value because no country has written laws that permit bribery. It should go without saying that if the actual exclusion written into the statute is of no practical value, its much looser, unwritten cousin is of even less value.

The idea that a bribe is legal because a foreign official accepted a payment overlooks the fundamental nature of bribery transactions: It takes two to tango.

You cannot have a successful bribery transaction without a government official accepting the bribe, but the fact that the official accepted does not mitigate your liability for the bribe. In addition, the excuse conflates the corrupt official with the foreign government writ large. Officials who accept a bribe are not making an official policy statement on behalf of their government in doing so. Indeed, in most cases what the officials are doing is illegal in their country too, and they know it. The fact that they may not get caught, or that such transactions are widespread in their country, does not render them any less illegal.

"It wasn't bribery—it was extortion!"

This excuse is usually offered up when the request for a bribe is accompanied by a threat of harm if the bribe is not paid. The harm may be explicit, implied, or merely perceived by the potential payer. Generally, the threat involves some kind of business harm and rarely involves a threat to the personal safety or health of the employee.

Traditionally, extortion involves three elements: (1) the coercion of some act (2) through a threat to do something illegal, accompanied by the perceived means to carry through on the threat, that (3) results in the transfer of property (typically money) from the victim to the one doing the threatening. Extortion is similar to robbery (where property is taken directly from a person through the use or threat of immediate force) and is distinguished from blackmail (where the threat is to do something that is perfectly legal, like exposing a fraud or informing someone's spouse of an affair).

When people claim they were extorted in the bribery context, they borrow the concept in an effort to paint themselves as a victim of a foreign official's criminal conduct ("He told me we wouldn't win the contract without paying him. I had no choice!"). But in doing so, they confuse the crime of extortion with the more general criminal defense of "duress." In almost all FCPA cases, neither extortion nor duress will work as defenses.

The idea behind these defenses is that people generally are not held criminally responsible for doing things that were not voluntary. To use either extortion or duress as a defense in an FCPA case, the bribe payer would have to show that the threat from the government official was so significant that the payment amounted to an *involuntary act*. That will never be easy to do.

The defense of duress will almost never be available for bribery because it requires the threat or use of physical force sufficient to cause death or serious bodily injury. This is why the bank teller who unlocks the safe when there is a gun to her head and allows the bank robber to escape with the money is not herself guilty of bank robbery. The teller's actions were made under duress—that is, without free will—and she cannot be held responsible for them. Similar facts will rarely arise in the bribery context.

Similarly, few threats in the extortion context will be so severe or immediate that they will operate to excuse bribery. Put another way, you may well be the victim of some mild form of extortion by a government official, but that fact alone does not excuse you from your own criminal act of violating the FCPA.

Perceived "extortion" for a bribe payment can happen in any number of ways. Perhaps you already have a contract to sell goods to a foreign government and just before the contract comes up for renewal, an official comes to you and says he will choose your competitor unless you agree to refund 3 percent of the contract price to him. (He may even suggest that you can raise your prices by 3 percent to offset this cost.) Or perhaps your factory is having tax problems and a local tax official tells you that your tax problems will be dealt with informally (rather than being elevated to the enforcement bureau in the capital), but only if you agree to purchase certain raw materials from a business she (or her relative) happens to own (often at an inflated price). "Otherwise," she says, "your tax problems may become very serious. If headquarters gets involved, I won't be able to help you."

It should be clear that neither example involves a threat of sufficient immediacy and severity that a payment to either official could be described as *involuntary*. Moreover, in both examples, *you* are not extorted because you can simply walk away. There might be a business consequence to your company if you walk away, but there is no consequence to *you*.

This distinction is important because the FCPA can be enforced against individuals and companies. Thus, paying a bribe to avoid some threatened harm to your company can mean criminal charges not only for the company but also for you.

The only historical example I know of where extortion is even discussed in the FCPA context is in the original legislative history of the FCPA. In that example, a foreign military unit threatens to blow up an oil rig unless it is paid off. Setting aside questions about whether such a scenario even implicates the FCPA (after all, the payment is not to obtain or retain business), the extreme nature of the example makes it clear that it is a little-used defense. Most bribes are not paid on an oil rig faced with dynamite.

As a manager, you will almost always have a choice about whether to pay a bribe. If you do not pay the bribe, there may be no consequence at all or, at most, some minor impact on your career because you fail to secure a contract. I would hope that any such impact could be mitigated by a candid conversation with your boss about why you walked away from a potential business deal.

In all but the most extreme cases, individual managers will never be able to show that a decision to commit a criminal FCPA violation was *involuntary* and, therefore, *not actionable*. In most cases, a foreign government official can make threats all day long, and most managers can simply get on a plane and go home.

CHAPTER 2

What's the Big Deal?

Billion-Dollar Fines and Jail Time

On its face, the FCPA sets out a variety of fines depending on who the violator is and the severity of the violation. For violating the anti-bribery provisions, an individual can be imprisoned for up to five years and fined up to $100,000 *per violation*. A company can be fined up to $2 million per violation (a company obviously cannot be thrown in jail). Anti-bribery violations can also result in debarment from bidding on public contracts or participating in public programs (which can be the death knell for businesses in certain industries, such as defense contracting or pharmaceuticals).

Violations of the books and records provisions are subject to a wide range of potential penalties, depending on the level of egregiousness and which agency is pursuing them. In civil actions brought by the SEC that involve negligent record keeping and nothing more, individuals can be punished by fines up to $5,000 per violation and companies up to $50,000 per violation. Intentional books and records violations are prosecuted criminally by the DOJ and result in fines of up to $5 million per violation and 20 years in prison for individuals and up to $25 million fines per violation for companies.

For an individual, the monetary penalties can be severe and the threat of jail time downright terrifying. For corporations, especially very large companies, fines for single violations may not look large, but looks can be deceiving.

In late 2008, Siemens, one of the best-known companies in the world, agreed to settle FCPA allegations with the DOJ and SEC for a total of $800 million. Notably, the settlement stated that the statutory calculus permitted a fine of up to *2.7 billion*, but that the government agreed to the lesser amount because of Siemens' substantial cooperation. (The basis for this reduction—the U.S. Sentencing Guidelines—is discussed in Chapter 12.) Incidentally, Siemens also paid its lawyers and forensic accountants many hundreds of millions more to conduct the investigation and reach the resolution with the government. On top of that, Siemens also paid German authorities more than $1 *billion* for the same conduct.

Only a few months later, the U.S. government obtained $579 million in fines and penalties against Halliburton and its former subsidiary, Kellogg, Brown & Root (KBR).

Since then, British weapons maker BAE Systems paid a $400 million fine, French telecom giant Alcatel-Lucent paid a $137 million fine, German auto conglomerate Daimler paid $200 million in fines and penalties, and the list goes on and on.

So, how exactly do you get from the penalties recited in the statute to the massive amounts in the *Siemens*, *Halliburton/KBR*, *BAE*, *Alcatel-Lucent*, and *Daimler* settlements? There are several ways:

1. Every instance of bribery or record-keeping violations can constitute a separate act for penalty purposes. In the case of any prolonged pattern of behavior (routine payments to authorities of any kind), it is easy to see how the fines can add up quickly.
2. The SEC always has the ability to seek disgorgement of any ill-gotten gains derived from the scheme, meaning any profit

made (or money saved) may have to be handed over to the U.S. government.

3. The DOJ can seek criminal penalties under the Alternative Minimum Fines Act, a statute that permits it to seek the maximum penalty under the statute or twice the benefit derived from the criminal act, whichever is more.

Each of these three can be combined to permit the government to seek huge fines, as it did against Siemens.

But the real lesson from the *Siemens* case is more subtle and much more important: The *Siemens* settlement—the biggest FCPA settlement in history—did not contain a single admission of bribery by the parent company.

Important Lessons from Siemens: They Don't Need to Prove Bribery—Books and Records Violations Are Enough

The *Siemens* settlement contains allegations that read like a spy novel. There are secret bank accounts around the world with hundreds of millions of dollars and euros channeled through them; funds funneled through layers of fictitious companies or joint ventures, the purposes for which growing more obscure with each transfer; payments to bogus bagmen disguised as "consultants," who ultimately handed money over to government officials all over the world in exchange for significant amounts of business; corporate insiders managing slush funds with a wink and a nod to their colleagues; illicit payoffs to secure contracts for everything from a power station renovation in Iraq, to the manufacturing of identity cards in Argentina, to mobile telephone contracts in Bangladesh. Some of this was revealed through records that were secreted away by individuals wanting protection in the form of proof that they did not act alone.

Ultimately, insiders turned on their employers when the pressure got too high and they faced individual criminal liability for what they had done

But despite the extreme facts, companies like KBR (though not KBR's former parent, Halliburton) pleaded guilty to criminal charges while Siemens only admitted to record-keeping and internal controls violations (although certain Siemens subsidiaries also pleaded to criminal conspiracy charges). Although U.S. authorities certainly could have pursued a criminal case against Siemens, in the end, the company did not admit to a single act of actual bribery. And yet, of the two cases, Siemens paid substantially more in fines to U.S. and German authorities than Halliburton/KBR did. Why?

The answer is complex but consists of a combination of intense cooperation by the company, good lawyering, and policy choices by the U.S. authorities. Companies facing potential prosecution for FCPA violations have a fundamental decision to make early on: to cooperate with the government or not. To be sure, as every American child learns, the burden of proof in a criminal case lies with the government, and the accused is generally under no obligation to actively help the prosecution. But the reality is that most legitimate companies choose to cooperate with government inquiries.

Generally, doing this means conducting a full, independent internal investigation, at its own expense, and handing the results of that investigation over to the government. Once that process concludes, the company and the government negotiate a resolution. The resolution can range anywhere from a criminal plea, large fine, and the imposition of an outside monitor to oversee the company's compliance to the government declining the case entirely and walking away.

The most common result, when a company conducts a thorough investigation and hands the results over, is that the government will agree to resolve the case with something short of a criminal plea in exchange for the company's continued cooperation with any additional investigation the government conducts. Short of a complete walk-away, a company usually will have to admit to at least *something*, and the less insidious books and records violations are the most common.

Although this process sounds simple enough, many companies radically underestimate the time, disruption, and cost of the process. Thorough investigations take months (sometimes years) to complete. Often hundreds of thousands or many millions of pages of documents will be reviewed. All employees involved in the relevant transactions will be subjected to detailed interviews by outside counsel, generally after counsel has reviewed all of the witness's emails and other documents. Each witness's explanation is compared to all others and every inconsistency is probed, often in rounds of follow-up interviews. The process can feel interminable and invasive, and, as an individual manager, you will have no visibility into the process and no idea what other witnesses and other documents say.

In exchange for undertaking this process and making the results available to the government for the government to use however it wants (e.g., to prosecute individuals), the company achieves a better resolution. This is a win-win for both sides. The company avoids much harsher criminal penalties and gets the matter resolved sooner than it otherwise would, and the government gets to collect a fine and gather evidence it might not have been able to gather on its own (such as corporate records from foreign countries).

With Siemens, hundreds of millions of dollars were spent investigating and reporting the results to various governments. In the end, although Siemens paid substantial fines, the company admitted to no bribery violations. This is crucial because not admitting to bribery violations allowed Siemens to avoid a debarment order that would have eliminated its ability to bid on

U.S. government contracts (a lucrative source of income, which might have killed the company had it been lost).

For its part, the U.S. government got its hands on a tremendous amount of valuable information, still collected the largest FCPA fine in history, and is now free to bring as many prosecutions of individuals or other companies as it likes based on the evidence obtained from Siemens, all with the full ongoing cooperation of Siemens and its directors and officers. Indeed, rumor has it that as many as 300 individuals came under some form of investigation by U.S. or German authorities in connection with the *Siemens* case.

There are three lessons to take away from this: (1) Companies really do get a break for full cooperation; (2) companies will turn on their own employees and throw them to the wolves in order to save themselves; and (3) the government is fully willing (and even expects) to take advantage of this dynamic.

Getting Thrown under the Bus: Understanding the Dynamics of Internal Investigations

Although it is an obvious statement, it bears repeating here: You are the only one looking out for you.

The dynamics at play in internal investigations are not concerned with your interests. The pressure on a company to reach a resolution is real and takes on a life of its own. Even on relatively innocent facts, individuals can find themselves out of a job and, even worse, out on their own and on the business end of a government investigation. Understanding how this happens is the key to understanding why, as a manager within such a company, compliance and reporting up the chain of command are central not only to corporate survival but to your own survival.

A well-choreographed dance goes on between companies, external auditors, the government, and the media in any FCPA investigation. Members of senior management and the board of directors have obligations to the company's shareholders. Among these is a fiduciary duty to care for the company's assets by ensuring that they are used and accounted for properly and that the company acts in a legal manner. Failure to meet these responsibilities can result their own personal liability for directors and officers. Even if they do not care about the FCPA—indeed, even if they think the law is stupid and should not be enforced at all—directors and senior officers care very much about themselves and their own potential liability for not taking the law seriously. Thus, members of boards and senior management—especially independent outside directors, who generally have no personal connection to the company and thus no deep or long-held allegiance to any of its employees—almost always decide that they need to conduct a full investigation of FCPA allegations and cooperate fully with the government.

In addition, the company's external auditors will want to be apprised of any criminal acts or acts of fraud discovered within the company, especially those that might involve false documentation or financial records. Failure to tell the external auditors such facts can have grave consequences if they are uncovered later; for example, they may cause the auditor to withdraw from the engagement and to publicly disavow prior financial statements it has audited. Such an event has catastrophic consequences for a public company and generally results in government investigation and a wave of lawsuits against both the company and its directors and officers (another reason why directors and officers opt for disclosure and investigation). In addition, future public filings will be delayed, which severely impacts a company's ability to raise capital and risks delisting from the stock market.

Once an investigation begins, the mandate from the top down is generally to find the truth and root out any wrongdoing.

That a company has taken an aggressive stance toward investigating and taking remedial action is something the government considers when deciding punishment. Because the directors and officers have their own personal liability to worry about, and because those obligations are owed to the shareholders and not to the company's employees, they are more than willing to sacrifice individual employees deemed responsible in some way for the greater good of saving the company (and themselves).

You can see where this is going.

The ones left out in the cold in the process just described are invariably the individual employees—especially lower and mid-level management—who often are the closest to the violations and, therefore, the easiest for the company to offer up as sacrificial lambs. What is worse, the individual managers generally have no control over what the company tells the government or what the government does with that information. As these pieces begin to fall into place, an entirely different dynamic begins to occur: the race to cooperate.

Prosecutors are fond of saying that the first ones in the door get the best deals. That is, the first manager who shows up and agrees to cooperate gets treated much better than the last manager who refuses to cooperate and dares the government to prosecute him or her. The truth of the matter is that the government has limited resources and cannot prosecute everyone. Another truth is that, all things being equal, a prosecutor would rather prove the easy case than the hard one. Thus, the person who cooperates early helps make an easy case against someone else. Often it takes awhile for a witness to blink and start cooperating, and the game is made more complex by the fact that people are often coy about what they are doing. But every good white-collar defense attorney knows how to play this game, and the race to cooperate can start surprisingly early.

Many managers resist this, but the pattern occurs over and over. Even among the closest business colleagues, personal relationships are abandoned with remarkable speed when people realize they potentially face personal criminal liability and the only defense they may have is to blame other people—even their old friends. When it comes to careers and livelihoods, no one is going to stick their neck out to save you, especially not a director or officer that you have never met (or have met only in passing).

When you find yourself in the crosshairs of an internal or government investigation, you generally learn very quickly that you are on your own. Those who delude themselves into thinking that their old friends within the company will protect them, vouch for them, or otherwise try to save them are the ones who often suffer the most.

A Little "CYA" Goes a Long Way

The best protection for individuals is compliance. Spot FCPA issues and report them up. In the chapters that follow, many common problems are discussed. When you see them, report them. That is the best protection you can have from later being accused of not following company policies, not taking issues seriously, being a negligent manager, or turning a blind eye to violations occurring right under your nose. Report it up. Save the emails. Follow up if there is no response. The best defense you can have when you are sitting across the table from someone like me is: "I kept raising the issue to the right people. What else do you want me to do?"

This simple act just might save your job (directors and officers generally are sympathetic to this argument) and keep you out of the government's sights (it is hard for the government to prove you are criminally responsible when you keep raising the issue instead of keeping it quiet). But more important, if things are working right in your company, spotting issues and reporting them up won't just give you a defense if you ever need one: It actually will result in FCPA compliance.

People Really Do Go to Jail

When David Kay and Douglas Murphy were indicted in 2001 for violating the FCPA—both while at American Rice, Inc.—the government's theory had never been fully tested in the courts. This is the kind of observation normally of interest only to a lawyer who cares about such things, but it is of particular practical interest to you because Kay and Murphy ultimately were convicted and went to prison based on that then-untested theory.

The theory was this: By paying Haitian customs officials to accept false bills of lading that understated the amount of rice being imported into Haiti, Kay and Murphy substantially reduced their employer's customs duties and sales tax obligations. That made the company's products more competitive in the marketplace, and that ultimately helped it to obtain or retain business in Haiti.

Sound like a stretch to you? It did to many FCPA observers at the time, too. Most people—including Kay's and Murphy's lawyers—argued that payments to reduce customs duties and sales taxes, while inappropriate, were not the kinds of payments "to obtain or retain business" that the FCPA is aimed at. Indeed, keeping tax liabilities as low as possible is a goal of all businesses, and in any event reduced taxes are related only theoretically to ultimately being more competitive and obtaining more business. If Congress intended the FCPA to reach these kinds of payments, it could have drafted the law specifically to do so, but it didn't. And most important, even if the courts were to read this into the law, Kay and Murphy certainly shouldn't be *criminally* responsible for adhering to an interpretation of the FCPA that no prior court had adopted. How could they have even known that their conduct violated the FCPA?

All good arguments, but Kay and Murphy lost. Kay went to prison for three years and Murphy for five. The theory pursued in their case is now widely accepted, and its impact reverberates through most of the chapters to follow.

The bottom line for our purposes here is that you need to understand how broadly the FCPA is applied. You need to understand its principles, not merely a rigid list of specific types of violations. Understanding the theory will help you think creatively about potential forms of bribery and how to spot potential issues. What the *Kay* decision (as it is known) tells you is that the novelty or obscurity of the issue does not provide a safe harbor. The government is creative with its theories of prosecution. You can go to jail for a type of violation that even FCPA lawyers would consider unique or novel.

The *Kay* decision marked the beginning of a tidal wave of FCPA enforcement that culminated in the *Siemens, Halliburton/KBR*, and other large settlements I mentioned earlier. The DOJ has pursued more FCPA cases in the last few years than in the entire *previous 30 years* of the statute's existence. This is due, in significant part, to the broad interpretation handed down in *Kay* and the related realization by corporations that it is safer to self-report potential FCPA violations to the DOJ and SEC (and give the government evidence and cooperation, as discussed earlier) than to wait for a government investigation and creative legal theory. Voluntary disclosures have become standard, even in cases where the violations are small, obscure, or somewhat novel.

With this surge in FCPA investigations against corporations has come a similar surge in individual prosecutions. Suddenly, actions against individuals have become far easier for the government to pursue thanks to the large amounts of evidence voluntarily given to prosecutors by corporations. For example, ex-KBR chief executive Jack Stanley pleaded guilty to FCPA charges in connection with the *Halliburton/KBR* matter and was imprisoned for more than seven years.

But jail time results from far less egregious cases. For example, two former employees of Control Components Incorporated (CCI), maker of industrial pump equipment, pleaded guilty to bribing employees of various state-owned energy companies. Unlike *Halliburton/KBR* or *Siemens*, the CCI pleas involved only about $1 million in payments spread over dozens of relatively small transactions. Importantly, the CCI director of Worldwide Sales was charged not only for approving certain payments but also for later denying that he did so to CCI's internal auditors and then instructing others to delete emails to conceal the payments. As has often been said, sometimes the cover-up is worse than the crime.

An even smaller example is that of Charles Edward Jumet, who, as an officer for a Virginia-based company, authorized $212,400 in payments to Panamanian officials to help his company obtain a maintenance contract for lighthouses and buoys in Panama. Jumet pleaded guilty to FCPA and conspiracy charges and was sentenced to 87 months in prison, slightly more than Jack Stanley's sentence in the *Halliburton/KBR* case. The point is: The bribes do not have to be huge to garner huge prison terms.

Indeed, in touting the DOJ's success in charging individuals with FCPA violations, Attorney General Eric Holder remarked in a May 31, 2010, speech to the Organisation for Economic Co-Operation and Development that, since 2004, the DOJ:

> *charged nearly 80 individuals. And the pace is accelerating. Let me be clear, prosecuting individuals is a cornerstone of our enforcement strategy because, as long as [bribery] remains a tactic, paying large monetary penalties cannot be viewed by the business community as merely "the cost of*

doing business." The risk of heading to prison for bribery is real, from the boardroom to the warehouse.[1]

While undoubtedly true, the actual statistics paint a slightly different picture. As of this writing, the most recent data available was that the average age of people in prison right now for FCPA violations is 58 years old. This single fact should send chills down the spine of any senior executive. What it tells you is this: Mid-level managers might lose their jobs and harm their careers, but senior executives implicated in bribery go to jail.

Many factors go into the calculus used by prosecutors to determine whether charges against individuals are warranted, but you should have no illusions that FCPA violations are "victimless" or purely "white collar" crimes that do not result in actual prison time. People go to jail, especially senior people with the power to stop violations when they learn of them. One of the goals of this book is to ensure that you will never become one of them.

Finally, recent legislation has added to the anticorruption onslaught. A little-noticed whistleblower provision in the 2010 financial reforms rewards individuals for tipping off the SEC to violations of U.S. securities laws, including the FCPA. Depending on the value of the information supplied to the SEC, whistle-blowers stand to recover between 10 and 30 percent of any amount the SEC recovers that exceeds $1,000,000. That's essentially a $100,000 *minimum* recovery in any action covered by the whistleblower statute. Given the *Siemens, Halliburton/KBR, BAE, Alcatel-Lucent,* and *Daimler* settlements discussed above, you can see that the recoveries are potentially much larger. The

---

[1]Full text available at www.justice.gov/ag/speeches/2010/ag-speech-100531.html.

existence of the whistleblower program makes good compliance all the more important. You want to stop violations before they occur because your employees may have less incentive to report FCPA violations to management. They may instead choose to report them directly to the SEC and put part of the recovery in their pocket.

CHAPTER 3

You Do More with the Government Than You Think

As the discussion of *Kay* should make clear, the FCPA is not focused on sales to government customers or sales at all, for that matter. If your company sells products or services directly to a foreign government, then those sales are an obvious area where you have FCPA compliance risks. You don't need to read this book to understand that. But even if your company does not sell directly to any foreign governments, you still interact with those governments on a regular basis. Just like the dealings with the Haitian customs officials in *Kay*, all of these interactions are fertile ground for potential FCPA violations, especially in countries where corruption is widespread.

To recap, although the FCPA prohibits all of the actions outlined in Chapter 1 if made "in order to assist" your company "in obtaining or retaining business ... or directing business to, any person," the *Kay* case upheld an extremely broad view of what counts as obtaining or retaining business. The "business nexus"—as lawyers call it—between the payment and any resulting business need only be slight.

That interpretation basically prohibits any payment or gift of "anything of value" intended to influence any foreign official's nontrivial actions in a way that benefits a company and its efforts to obtain or retain business. This broad definition reaches a vast array of payments. Some of the most common are payments that permit a company to skirt regulatory requirements, illegally lower its taxes or customs duties, obtain licenses or permits without going through the proper procedure, or influence government specifications for products. Each of the most common problem areas are discussed in detail in this chapter.

At the outset, though, note that the kinds of regulatory violations discussed in this chapter all warrant more general observations that I and many others have made: An act of bribery generally does not occur in isolation. Corruption is a state of mind. Where one corrupt official exists, there are usually others. Where corruption is cultural, it is also systemic. This reality generally has ramifications on the other side of transactions, as well. In other words, a company rarely engages in only a single act of bribery. Where one act is committed, there are generally more.

There may well be patterns. Often corrupt payments will be localized within a specific country or region or within a specific division of a company whose business necessitates more government interaction. Where a particularly rogue employee exists, corrupt payments will be clustered around that individual's activity (or the activity of the individual's group, region, or division). But rarely is there only a single act.

Interactions with Customs

Every company doing business internationally deals with customs, both in the United States and abroad, on a regular basis. For companies with overseas manufacturing facilities, customs transactions occur in high volume. Each time raw materials come into the country or goods flow out, there is a customs transaction. Often there are many transactions each day and hundreds or thousands each month in each overseas business unit. In very large companies, with widespread, global manufacturing facilities, there can be tens of thousands of monthly customs transactions.

Each transaction impacts the company's ability to conduct its business—by getting raw materials to the factory, getting goods into distribution channels or directly to a customer, or getting essential equipment and supplies where they are needed—and, therefore, every company has a strong incentive to ensure that these customs transactions go smoothly. Each transaction involves a payment to the government. And each transaction involves a regulatory process that includes a variety of technical compliance issues, from proper paperwork, to inspections, to duty calculations and tax payments. As a result, each customs transaction contains FCPA risk.

If this sounds overblown, first consider that *Kay* itself was essentially a customs case. Second, consider the U.S. government's global investigation of Panalpina, one of the world's most prominent and well-known customs clearance firms. Many international companies outsource their customs clearance work to third parties, such as Panalpina, and the use of agents or other third parties for these and many other services is its own distinct issue that is covered in detail in Chapter 8. But for now, the Panalpina series of investigations illustrates just how high risk customs clearance is and how seriously U.S. authorities take it. For every company that outsources its customs clearance, there is another that handles it in-house. It makes no difference whether an agent is used or not. Any company can commit these same violations just as easily through its own in-house customs clearance personnel.

The global Panalpina investigations grew out of previous FCPA cases involving ABB Vetco Gray, Inc., Aibel Group Limited, and others in the oil business in Nigeria. In the course of those prior cases, U.S. authorities became suspicious of Panalpina and began an investigation. That investigation grew into a global investigation of other companies that used Panalpina. In the summer of 2007, the U.S. Department of Justice sent out document requests to approximately a dozen other companies, asking each of them about their dealings with Panalpina in countries around the world. In the course of doing so, the U.S. government not only kicked off a massive investigation of Panalpina itself but also of each of the companies to which the letters were sent. As will be discussed in Chapter 8, actions of the agent can be imputed to the principal. For that reason, each company that employed Panalpina was potentially on the hook for any illegal actions taken by Panalpina on its behalf.

Both in the Panalpina cases and in other matters, the same kinds of customs issues come up over and over. I generally place them into three categories, each of which can occur in isolation or in various combinations within a single customs transaction: (1) payments to reduce customs duties; (2) payments to skip inspection or paperwork requirements; and (3) payments to overlook regulatory violations or stop investigations into those violations (which I address in the next section on tax issues and again at the end of the chapter).

Issue 1: Payments to Reduce Duties

The *Kay* case involved the reduction of duties. This is a routine problem throughout the world. I have seen it in Africa, the Middle East, Asia, and South America. Often these violations are surprisingly well documented because whoever is doing it—whether an in-house person or a customs clearance agent—keeps a good record of how much money he or she is saving the company. In this person's mind, it's proof of a job well done. In the hands of the U.S. government, it can be proof of a federal crime.

False duty reductions generally happen either through outright falsification of bills of lading and other records, which understate the value or quantity of goods in the shipment, or through a false classification of the goods into a customs category that is subject to a lower duty. Although it is certainly possible for either of these techniques to be successful without the aid of any government officials, systematic use of either method generally requires collusion with a customs official. With a high volume of transactions, it's really only a matter of time before you get caught, unless you have the cooperation of the relevant officials. The best way to ensure that you don't get caught is to ensure that the customs official to whom the documentation is presented is in on the scheme.

Issue 2: Paying to Minimize Inspections

The second category of potential customs violations involves the speed with which goods and equipment are cleared through customs. Unlike presenting false documents to reduce duties, which most people see as obviously problematic, speeding up the processing by sidestepping inspections or paperwork is a tougher issue. Under certain circumstances, these payments can be perfectly legal. As discussed in Chapter 9, if all that the payment does is move the payer to the front of the inspection line, the payment may be a facilitating payment, which is perfectly legal under the FCPA (although it may still be illegal under local laws or other potentially applicable laws, such as the U.K. Bribery Act). But the point here is merely that it is often difficult to make this determination.

As discussed in the Chapter 1 hypothetical involving the Indian customs broker who conducted an "intervention" that magically whisked the new equipment through an otherwise glacial bureaucratic process, often more is skipped than just the line. Required paperwork and inspections also disappear along with the wait. Indeed, this was one of the very issues in the cases that led to the Panalpina investigations. Before paying to move goods through customs on an expedited basis, run the payment past someone who deals with these questions routinely. If that is not practical (as it sometimes won't be), you will want to be able to document that all other applicable requirements were followed in clearing the goods. In practice, you'll often find that the effort to document compliance is so burdensome that it is easier simply to wait for the normal process to run its course.

Sometimes problems are not just with one-time interventions but with special statuses granted to companies in some countries—a status that allows routine passage through customs without going through the normal customs process. These statuses take on many names in different countries. In some countries, it is a perfectly legitimate status granted to highly compliant companies by a customs regime that needs to clear its backlog. In other countries, it is an illegitimate status granted to anyone willing to pay enough to buy his or her way out of having to comply with the law. You probably will not be able to tell the difference when you come across these situations in real life. When you see one, report it to the compliance people within your company.

Issue 3: Ensuring Violations Are Overlooked

The third type of customs issue is not unique to customs interactions. Making payments to overlook or "unofficially" settle regulatory violations arises in any regulatory context. If alleged violations are resolved by paying a cash "fine" directly to the official who found the violation, without any paperwork or formal reports, you may want to undertake an effort to understand these transactions. The "fine" may be something more suspicious.

Because large multinational companies typically have a high volume of customs transactions and the standard transaction is relatively small, FCPA violations in these transactions can be difficult to spot. As a manager who is not mired in the granular detail of particular customs transactions, you are unlikely to discover violations unless someone tells you about them. This is why it is crucial to understand how the import/export process works in the countries where you have responsibilities. Often asking simple questions to the relevant employees will yield all of the information you need. How do we ensure our goods aren't held up by customs? What exactly is each of the line items on the customs broker's invoice for? Are there administrative fees or service charges that seem duplicative or excessive? These are good places to start. Ask these questions, and you might be surprised by the answers.

Interactions with Tax Authorities

Interactions with tax authorities present many of the same risks as customs interactions, and often, tax and customs problems go hand in hand. The central distinction between typical interactions with tax and customs authorities is that customs transactions are often very low dollar and very high volume. Tax transactions are often the opposite. They occur less frequently, but the dollars at issue are much larger. Large transactions directly with government officials are always high-risk transactions when you are doing business in a country known for corruption.

Businesses at high risk for substantial overlap between customs and tax issues are those that have manufacturing facilities in special "bonded" or duty-free zones. That encompasses virtually every major international company with operations in China, Vietnam, Malaysia, Indonesia, India, Dubai, Egypt, Morocco, Brazil, Peru, and Mexico.

Let's take a complex yet all too common example. You have a manufacturing facility in southern China where you make products primarily destined for overseas customers. Raw materials are shipped into the factory from Hong Kong, goods are made at the facility, and they are shipped back out. At least that's how it is supposed to work. When it does, the manufacturing arrangement entitles you to preferential tax treatment in China. All imports to the facility and all international exports from the facility are tax and duty free.

But at least some goods are sold locally, and on those sales you owe both duties and taxes. Furthermore, local law requires complete segregation of raw materials destined for use in manufacturing goods for local sales. On top of that, goods manufactured for local sales are supposed to be manufactured on separate, segregated machines that manufacture only goods to be sold locally (and, of course, those machines were supposed to be subject to import duties when you installed them in the factory). Thus, although you can have local sales, you essentially have to establish a separate factory and warehouse facility within your larger international operation and maintain meticulous records accounting for the import, storage, use, and sale of all of those raw materials and goods.

But, as a practical matter, the company may have no segregation at all. And meticulous records? Hardly.

And then the tax inspectors show up for a surprise inspection of the company's books. It takes them little time to figure out that your records are poor, that you have only a rough idea of your local sales, and that you likely have vastly underpaid the applicable taxes on those sales. The inspectors go out into the warehouse and discover no segregation of materials or equipment. The tax inspectors call the customs inspectors and say something that roughly translates as "Get a load of this!"

The jig, as they say, is up.

This is primo bribery territory. If you are a fairly senior regional manager, you might never even learn about this debacle because the petty cash safe will be emptied out and the local factory manager might do everything possible to ensure the tax and customs inspectors look the other way. If you are closer to the problem, you need to be extremely wary of any local employee who tells you not to worry about the inspectors, that she will smooth everything over. Worst of all, if you are a manager and actually are aware of systemic problems like these, especially if they are widespread and long standing, you have to ask yourself, "How is it that they have gotten away with this for so long?" If an inspection does occur and nothing comes of it, you need to raise some serious questions about how exactly the company managed to avoid getting severely fined or even shut down.

Not all interactions raise issues as serious and immediate as the ones just discussed, but even much more routine interactions with tax authorities are fraught with risk. For example, the most widely used tax scheme in the world is the value-added tax (VAT). Often VAT is collected on raw materials before they are incorporated into manufactured goods. In many cases, when those goods are sold later under some form of tax-free regime, the company can apply for a refund of the VAT previously paid on the raw materials.

But to receive the refund, the company and the tax official must reach an agreement about the refund amount, and then the official must approve the refund for processing and payment. One common way to ensure the amount is agreed to and speedily approved and processed is to pay the official a commission equal to a percentage of the refund. Often the commission is paid to the official in cash after the VAT refund has been received by the company. In these cases, local management usually tries to defend the commissions as facilitating payments intended only to ensure quick processing.

For reasons discussed in detail in Chapter 9, these transactions cannot be defended as facilitating payments. To begin with, the amounts paid are often too large to pass the smell test. Beyond that, the official making the determination about the refund request generally is making a series of discretionary judgment calls about what qualifies for the refund, how it should be calculated, and even whether certain issues warrant further discussion with his superiors. The commission removes these variables from the equation.

Although many tax theorists claim that the VAT is the most *fair* tax regime as a matter of public policy, the practical realities of implementing a VAT scheme underscore the vast gulf between theory and practice. At the end of the day, a VAT system is highly bureaucratic, resulting in many interactions with tax officials and many opportunities for improper payments. If you have responsibility for a business in a high-risk jurisdiction subject to a VAT regime, make sure you have a handle on who interacts with the tax officials, in what capacity, and concerning what kinds of issues.

Licensing, Inspections, and Specifications

Of course, there are many other areas where you deal with the government besides tax and customs. Each of them presents risks. I'll walk briefly through some of those areas and risks now. Obviously, this list isn't exhaustive, but all of the examples to be discussed are common problems. Be on the lookout for these and other analogous situations.

Licenses and Permits

First off, pretty much everywhere in the world that you would want to do business requires that you obtain some kind of license to do so. Beyond just the mere right to open for business, these initial licenses often contain other provisions that can govern the way you do business for long periods of time. For example, the license may specify only certain kinds of activities or uses, thereby limiting your ability to expand or modify your business plan. It may specify the number or percentage of employees who can be expatriates, thereby limiting your ability to fill key management roles with experienced and trusted personnel from the company's foreign offices. It may specify particular types of equipment. It might specify the location of your factory or even incorporate specific plans for how the space is to be used (perhaps 70 percent of the square footage for manufacturing and 30 percent for administrative offices), thereby imposing artificial limits on your growth and flexibility. It may specify what percentage of your sales can be domestic or international. These kinds of restrictions all impose rigid limitations on your ability to run your business. Getting such restrictions modified or completely removed at the front end is highly valuable.

Generally, the best time to get these licenses modified is during the application phase, before they are set in stone. In high-corruption countries, many restrictions can be modified or removed for a price. Often the desire to modify the restrictions will be combined with a desire to get the application approved quickly and may be viewed by local personnel or consultants as a mere facilitating payment. But as we have seen, speedy processing combined with discretionary modifications to the process or the substantive requirements is not a facilitating payment at all.

Chapter 8 discusses the dangers of consultants in detail, but here it is worth noting that companies often place heavy reliance on local consultants during the start-up phase in a new country because they do not have any local personnel. In some countries, you cannot get a work visa for an employee without having a local company already established. In these instances, companies are faced with the Hobson's choice of either having their people in the country illegally while they set up the business, or placing heavy reliance on a local consultant to do the bulk of the initial legwork. But despite representations they might make, many local consultants know nothing about the FCPA and view the bribes paid in exchange for your licenses, complete with whatever terms you desire, as a routine and acceptable way of doing business. Once the basic business licenses are obtained, many other permits also may be required for everything from the trucks in the yard, to the heavy machinery on the factory floor, to the factory workers themselves.

Many of these licenses pose similar risks. In each instance, it is crucial that you have an understanding of what the applicable rules and restrictions are so that you will know whether your consultant or employee is obtaining something you are entitled to or some exception to the standard rules that will be difficult to explain after the fact, especially if accompanied by a payment of some kind. If you do not know what you are supposed to receive, you have no way of determining whether you are getting special treatment or not.

A blasé attitude toward obtaining licenses can have serious personal consequences. For example, Bobby Benton, a former vice president for a major offshore drilling rig operator, probably never dreamed that the U.S. government would bring a case against him. He is accused of approving one $10,000 payment made to ensure that a permit for a supply boat was not held up due to certain deficiencies in the equipment. He also is accused of taking certain steps to conceal a $15,000 payment made through one of his company's Mexican subsidiaries to ensure that the importation of a drilling rig was not held up due to customs delays.

Knowing nothing of the facts beyond the public disclosures, I can only speculate how much Benton really understood about the licensing and customs processes at issue in these two instances. But I have had many executives tell me that the customs or permitting processes in the countries where they operate are "nitpicky" or that "a $1 million piece of equipment" will be held up by a "low-level" inspector who is looking for any minor thing he can find just to hold them up and harass them. In these circumstances (just as in the customs example discussed in Chapter 1), often an agent can be found who can make the problems go away. When these situations present themselves, ask hard questions, demand proof that the process being described really is legitimate, get copies of the local regulations that allow for it, and file them away with the payment voucher. Do not end up where Bobby Benton ended up.

Work Permits and Visas

Work permits and visas are another area of concern. Often your expat workers are essential to the business unit's success, and they are almost always subject to special, and sometimes very obtuse, visa requirements. In addition, many companies use third-party services to obtain visas for their workers, which only add to the lack of transparency surrounding the process of obtaining them. Here again it is important to know what the local rules are so you can determine whether your agent is complying with them or skipping them. For example, is the applicant supposed to go down to the visa office in person so the officer can confirm that the picture on the application matches the person applying? This is a common requirement, and I have had many people tell me that when they use a third-party service, they do not have to waste a day going down to the immigration office. Indeed, many U.S. citizens use a third-party visa service overseas specifically *because* it gets them out of this requirement. Yet most of them could not imagine being able simply to get out of such a requirement with U.S. immigration officials. How do you think the third-party visa processor is able to avoid this cumbersome inspection requirement? If you are paying the third party for this convenience, the third party may well be paying someone down at the visa office to overlook the requirement.

Examples like this strike people as simply too petty to really be FCPA problems. Surely, they say, the DOJ or SEC is not bringing cases based on how people get their expat work permits in India or the Philippines. But recently, defense contractor DynCorp International disclosed that some of its subcontractors around the world might have paid as much as $300,000 to obtain visas and licenses and that those payments might have violated the FCPA. As of this writing, the U.S. government has not brought charges or extracted a settlement, but for our purposes here, the more important fact might be that DynCorp terminated its executive counsel and chief compliance officer (a position *above* the general counsel in the DynCorp organization) at approximately the same time as the announcement. Although the company did not say the two were connected, the media coverage about the case assumed that they were.

One of the first thematic points from Chapter 1 was that *FCPA violations rarely occur in isolation.* An FCPA case isn't ever going to be about the handful of work permits that were obtained through a visa processor who got your people out of inconvenient administrative requirements. It's going to be about that, and the customs issues, and the kickbacks to the tax official to get the VAT refund processed, as well as all of the other inspections, permits, and other regulatory requirements your company has been able to skirt or skip because of a steady stream of small payments, gifts, meals, or entertainment. Taken as a whole, this picture may be one of a U.S. company that does not "do business" with the host country's government at all (it makes no sales to the foreign government) but nonetheless is able to continue doing business in that country only through a continuous flow of graft that keeps the regulatory requirements light and the regulators very friendly.

Inspections and Certifications

Consider the many other areas that play a part in building this very cynical picture. What about the periodic health and safety inspections your plant always seems to pass? How does your factory manager always manage to escape without even the slightest ding or blemish on the inspection report? In fact, as the manager, have you ever even seen an inspection report? Do the inspectors even bother to draft one? Are they taken to lunch after the inspection? Can you imagine having the same relationship with the Occupational Safety and Health Administration inspectors in the United States?

These same questions apply to the environmental pollution inspectors, the equipment and vehicle inspectors, and all product inspections that occur in any kind of highly regulated industry. Think about pharmaceuticals; medical devices; sensitive equipment manufacturers; anything made for military use; and equipment in industries where a government is often involved, such as oil, mining, or communications. All of these areas generally have additional layers of inspections and certifications requiring additional contact with the local government. The only way to protect yourself and your company is to understand what the requirements are and how your local people deal with them. Simply relying on local employees to handle these issues because they "know how business is done" is a high-risk proposition.

One good study of the risks of relying on local people comes from the aforementioned Panalpina cases. In those cases, oil drilling and oil services contractors were engaged by oil companies in many countries. Often the contracts were for a period of several years, and the equipment involved—including drilling rigs—was expensive and cumbersome to dismantle and move.

When companies brought their equipment into the relevant countries, they faced a fundamental choice: permanently import it into the country, or import it on a temporary basis. Because almost no one expected the equipment to remain in these countries permanently, the temporary import regime made the most sense for many companies. Theoretically, a temporary import permit requires payment of duties only for the value of the equipment "used" during the period of the permit. Thus, companies saved huge amounts of importation duties and did not have to deal with formally exporting the equipment when they eventually wanted to move it to some other part of the world.

Although temporary import regimes exist all over the world, each country's model is different. To deal with these issues, these companies engaged Panalpina, a worldwide logistics provider and generally well-known and well-respected company. Panalpina had customs agents on the ground in these countries who could take care of the process of getting the temporary import permits. As you might imagine, with Panalpina engaged to take care of everything, often no one at the drilling or oil services companies paid much attention to what it was doing to obtain the permits.

If we pause here for a bit of reflection, on one hand I imagine that you can see exactly how and why such work would be outsourced. Indeed, it makes perfect sense. A company is going into a new country, it doesn't know the regulatory landscape, so it hires a well-known customs broker to take care of this issue and make sure things are done right. But the U.S. government undertook a global investigation of Panalpina and, ultimately, many companies that used Panalpina. The point is that these cases are actually pursued. Companies that used Panalpina were drawn into massive investigations simply because of a connection with a tainted agent that handled their freight forwarding and customs brokerage.

The allegations giving rise to the wave of Panalpina cases came from a series of related cases involving ABB Vetco Gray, Inc. that included allegations against "Agent A" (who was later revealed to be Panalpina). The allegations against Agent A were that it conspired with in-country employees of various companies to induce Nigerian customs officials "to provide preferential treatment in the customs clearance process and thereby secure an improper advantage with respect to the importation of goods and equipment into Nigeria." Specifically, they were alleged to have made payments to Nigerian customs officials when "goods and equipment were improperly or illegally imported," "documentation for imported goods were not in order," "there were delays" or "infractions of Nigerian customs laws were committed"—all of which would be invoiced as "local processing fees," "interventions," "express courier services," "evacuations" or other vague yet official-sounding terms (all of which come directly from the settlement documents).

As a manager, it is tempting to assume that everything is fine in any transaction involving outsourced services like these. But Aibel Group employees paid Panalpina $2.1 million over 61 transactions (about $34,400 on average), under the arrangements just outlined. Ask yourself if you really could explain an invoice for $20,000, $40,000, or $100,000 that merely contained the terms just recited without any additional description of the actual work performed. Sure, it may be from a well-known company, but how comfortable can you be that everything is legitimate if you have no other information?

To be clear, not having a solid understanding of what the funds were used for is a far cry from knowing, or even having reason to believe, that someone was paying bribes with the money, but the point here is that second-guessing after the fact leads to this kind of speculation. And, as we already have discussed, the DOJ and SEC don't need to prove bribes were paid to bring a case. Internal controls or record-keeping problems are enough. As a manager, you would be much better off to avoid getting caught in the middle of that kind of guessing game, and one of the best ways to do that is to have some understanding of the regulatory processes applicable to your business.

Barring the ability to gain an actual understanding of the regulatory process, you want to have a sensitivity to certain patterns that can occur. Any time your own people are, or an agent is, interacting with government officials on the company's behalf and the nature of the transaction cannot be clearly explained, something may be wrong. When you hear that the amount of the regulatory fees may change or is not set in stone, when you hear that there are delays because the personnel at the government office changed, when someone tells you that earlier problems or delays have disappeared because of special procedures with additional fees, you should ask questions. Generally, regulatory processes do not work this way.

Think of your own experiences with licensing something. When you go to the Department of Motor Vehicles (DMV), there is a chart of fees for the various services and permits. You wait in line, you fill out the required paperwork, you pay the fee, and you get the license. It is a straightforward process even if sometimes tedious or aggravating. Nothing changes in the middle of the transaction. It doesn't matter if the person who gave you the paperwork goes to lunch and a different individual receives and processes it. The fee doesn't change depending on whom you are dealing with.

When a permitting or licensing process begins to feel like someone is making it up as they go along, that is a sign that something may be wrong. Admittedly, many regulatory transactions are more complex than a trip to the DMV, but the complexities generally do not involve issues such as whether you'll be dealing with the same official throughout the transaction or what the calculus for determining the fee will be. If you are dealing with a real, legitimate process, the process itself generally will be known and understandable. Ensuring that you know and understand those processes goes a long way toward ensuring that you can spot a problematic transaction when one comes along.

The original *ABB Vetco Gray* matters that spawned the Panalpina cases dealt with transactions reflected on invoices that probably looked just fine to senior-level managers at the companies involved. But once those invoices and the under-lying transactions came under scrutiny, that same scrutiny was brought to bear on all prior transactions, not just the one that caught everyone's attention in the first place. Indeed, more than a dozen other companies were then drawn into multiyear investigations centering on their dealings with Panalpina. FCPA risk in connection with otherwise routine regulatory transactions is very real.

Bid and Tender Processes

One final regulatory example involves bid and tender processes, particularly where prospective bidders participate in setting the specifications for the tenders. Bid rigging in government contracts is illegal everywhere and is a subject most people inherently recognize as problematic. But a more subtle form can occur when an industry participates in helping a government set specifications for specific projects or for industry-wide applications to be used as standards in future projects.

It is of course common for government bodies to solicit input from relevant industry participants when setting specifications. This input can come in many forms, some legitimate and some not. Telling the difference is tough, but knowing the kinds of situations where lines can be crossed will help you ensure that your people do not inadvertently cross the line. The general rule is the more direct and sustained the contact with the relevant officials, the higher the risk.

Thus, a situation where the foreign government posts proposed rules, and the company submits written comments to be considered by the government in forming the final rules would pose no risk since there is no personal contact with any officials. Preparing a complex bid over a long period of time involving numerous meetings with relevant foreign officials, tours of plants or proposed construction sites, and even negotiations over exactly what the government wants or thinks it wants and how your company's products or services fit the bill pose the highest risks. In these scenarios, often there are many opportunities for the kinds of violations discussed in the next chapters to occur. Many times every single type of violation can crop up in a single series of negotiations. You buy lunches or dinners for the relevant officials during long days of meetings, you pick up their travel expenses when they visit your factory or research facility, you agree to utilize other companies or consultants recommended by the officials for relevant services as part of your bid package. At every turn there could be an FCPA problem.

Let's take one concrete example. You work for a firm trying to get a piece of a large infrastructure project in a foreign country. It is known in the industry that a tender process will begin in the next six months so you set up a meeting with the officials responsible for the project to discuss the project in general terms to get a sense of what you will need to do to prepare your bid. You know your competitors are setting up the same kinds of meetings.

At the meeting it becomes clear that the officials do not fully understand your industry's technology. You see an opportunity to freeze your competitors out if you can influence the officials to draft the specifications for the project in such a way that only your products (or perhaps products made using technology on which you hold the patents) will satisfy the requirements. You offer a follow-up meeting to provide general industry background, which they accept. Then you offer to host them at your plant to show them your technology, hoping to demonstrate how superior it is. Perhaps you even fly them to the United States so they can meet with the real experts at your research and development facility. Of course, some meetings are held at off-site locations, like a resort, with a round of golf and a nice dinner thrown in. On the trip to the United States you take the foreign officials sightseeing. Since they are going to be gone so long, you may even offer to fly their families to the United States, too, and arrange for a few days in Los Angeles so their kids can visit Disneyland, which would make the business trip a family vacation.

After all of this, the officials draft the project specifications so that only products exactly like yours will satisfy the tender. Perhaps they do so without even realizing that they have effectively undermined the bidding process because yours is the only company that can possibly satisfy the bid requirements.

No surprise that you win the contract at the end of the bidding.

Some of what has just been described may be permissible. Some of it is clearly not. Over the next few chapters it will become clear where the obvious and less obvious problems are. The main point here is that these and similar situations come up all the time, even in much more mundane scenarios. In fact, in the CCI case mentioned in the last chapter, one of the factual allegations supporting the charges was that CCI employees formed close relationships with influential insiders (euphemistically called friends-in-camp) who—in the words of the CCI plea agreement—"had the authority either to award contracts to CCI or influence the technical specifications of an order in a manner that would favor CCI."

Although beyond the scope of this book, the CCI case also broke new ground in that the DOJ charged the company with violating another statute—the Travel Act—for making payments and providing gifts to overseas "friends-in-camp" at wholly *private* companies because such payments violated California's seldom used commercial bribery statute. At the time of writing, the use of state commercial anti-bribery laws as a predicate offense for Travel Act violations had by no means become a trend. But the existence of similar laws in many states certainly raises the ominous prospect of more widespread use to prosecute bribery of wholly private, nongovernmental companies.

Furthermore, the recent enactment of the U.K. Bribery Act, which also governs commercial bribery (and is discussed in later chapters), is another example of this trend toward more expansive anti-bribery efforts.

Reducing Fines and Stopping Government Investigations

One final common area to watch for in your routine interactions with government officials is what happens when there is a regulatory violation of some kind. Such things are inevitable in any operation. No business unit gets everything right all the time. The corollary to this fundamental reality is a rule you should live by: Be suspicious of perfection. The absolute nonexistence of any regulatory violations is itself a red flag.

Any dynamic business unit of any size is going to have the occasional paperwork problem, late tax payment, expired expat work permit, health and safety violation, expired license on a piece of a equipment, or any of a hundred other things. If you find yourself managing a department, factory, or business unit that has never had any issues whatsoever, you need to ask yourself why. Is that really possible? Does that comport with your experience of the world generally? Are you really in charge of the one business in the world that operates flawlessly? This is a fair question to ask yourself if you run a business in Indiana, but it should set off flashing lights and sirens if you run a business in Indonesia or some other developing country.

The more corrupt the country, the more concern you should have. Corruption and bureaucracy go hand in hand. The more layers of government, the more red tape, the more officials you deal with, the more opportunities for corruption. Indeed, in many corrupt countries, low-level officials heavily subsidize their incomes through shakedowns, generally in the form of holding up routine processes or, in the case of those with regulatory inspection duties, finding violations anywhere and everywhere they can. If no inspector ever finds any violations of any kind in your facility, there may be only one reason why.

Your suspicion level should go up even further in cases where you are personally aware of regulatory problems. Let's go back to the example from earlier in this chapter where we had local and international sales within the same facility in a tax-free manufacturing zone. The regulatory requirement in that example was that materials and manufacturing machines be segregated between domestic and international sales, but in fact little or no segregation occurred. In cases like this, it might be common for a new manager to show up and, relatively early on, gain an understanding from the factory manager that the company has long had this problem but has been unable to address it properly. There may be legitimate reasons for this. Perhaps there are no machines available to have designated ones for local sales, or the machines are prohibitively expensive to acquire. (Often this excuse is a result of local management not wanting to ruin its numbers and not adequately explaining the basis of the requirements to upper management.) Or maybe the original business license did not anticipate the kind or amount of local business you now conduct.

When you learn of long-standing regulatory violations, you have to ask yourself the flip side of our fundamental rule: How have they gotten away with it for so long? These situations generally require passing the issue on to your compliance or internal audit departments. In these situations, when you look hard enough, you generally find the kinds of "relationship" expenses being incurred that result in very thorny problems. These are discussed in detail in subsequent chapters, but when the inspectors are being taken to lunch or dinner, given gifts at holiday times, or otherwise being entertained by your people, there will be some difficult questions to answer.

A Note on Foreign Litigation

One parting note relates to the employment of foreign counsel and their interactions with foreign judges. Litigation is a fact of life not just in the United States but increasingly throughout the world. U.S. companies may not fully appreciate how different the systems of justice are in other countries. I routinely see matters where local counsel is engaged based on a recommendation from another lawyer or a business acquaintance who may have used the counsel in the past. Often an initial conversation is had and an engagement letter signed, and the local counsel is off and running with little, if any, diligence done in connection with the engagement.

What few people seem to realize is how prevalent, and even standard, bribery of foreign judges is. Indeed, it may be such a routine part of the local litigation practice that being well known for paying bribes may have no affect on a local lawyer's reputation. The problem is that almost no U.S. lawyers would ever consider paying a bribe to a judge. Thus, it does not occur to them even to consider that their local counsel might have a different view on the subject. But lawyers pay bribes as a matter of course in other parts of the world. I had a case recently where a lawyer acted as the bagman and handed the bribe money to the foreign official (although not to a judge in that case). These things really do happen.

Suffice it to say that foreign judges are foreign officials under the FCPA. You should never assume that simply because someone is acting as your attorney in a foreign country that that person is above reproach. Frank conversations at the outset of any engagement may help to ensure that any bribery practices that may be routine in local litigation are not carried out on your company's behalf.

CHAPTER 4

Know Your Customers and Suppliers

The Dangers of State-Owned Entities

As discussed in Chapter 1, the FCPA prohibits bribes to employees of foreign government "instrumentalities." This means that all of the issues discussed in the chapters that follow apply with equal force to traditional governmental entities and to these instrumentalities. So what is an instrumentality of a foreign government?

In a nutshell, it is anything owned or controlled by the foreign government. This is an extremely broad category. There is no set threshold for "ownership," but it clearly includes anything in which the foreign government holds a 50 percent or greater stake. U.S. enforcement authorities generally take the position that the ownership interest would have to be much lower than 50 percent for a credible argument to be made that the government ownership interest is so negligible that, as a matter of law, the entity does not qualify as an instrumentality. Therefore, a cautious rule of thumb to apply is that if you learn of *any* government ownership of a company you deal with, you should assume it is an instrumentality until proven otherwise. To look at this problem from another angle, consider this: Many people who are foreign officials under the FCPA *have no idea that they are foreign officials* and would never describe themselves that way if asked.

One corollary to the state-owned entity problem is the issue of companies that are owned in whole or in part by individual government officials. Although such companies might not technically be "instrumentalities" under the FCPA, they raise similar issues and are examined in detail at the end of this chapter. In certain circumstances, the mere act of doing business with a company owned by a government official can be viewed as a gift to that official. In those cases position to help your business, you

JV

Of course, when the foreign control over an entity, there does ment ownership at all. This issue comes up in certain highly regulated industries where "private" companies or joint ventures permitted to operate within those industries effectively are controlled by the foreign government because it dominates the industry itself. Certain industries are notorious for government domination, such as oil and other natural resources, telecommunications, security and defense, large-scale infrastructure of any kind, and healthcare. If you operate in any of these industries, you need to be vigilant in spotting state-controlled entities.

Ownership and control issues are especially pronounced in any communist country and any other country with a formerly centralized economy. Thus, current communist regimes, such as China and Vietnam, present the same kinds of issues as former Soviet republics such as Kazakhstan or Uzbekistan. Many South American and Middle Eastern countries present similar issues because of either quasi-communist or socialist forms of government or traditionally heavy state involvement in all, or at least key, aspects of their economies. Although there have been significant efforts at privatization in many of these countries—including China and Vietnam—you will need to understand who you are dealing with because many state-owned entities that look and feel exactly like private companies are in fact instrumentalities for FCPA purposes.

The bottom line is that you have to know your customer or vendor before you know whether the FCPA's restrictions apply. This is not easy. And the question is not limited only to entities from which you get business. Anyone with whom you do business can cause problems. This includes all of your suppliers and service providers. After all, your suppliers and service providers make a profit from the business you give them. If that profit flows into the hands of individual officials, you need to be careful.

Privatization of Former Government Agencies or Companies

Let me get a common misconception out of the way right up front. Just because a company has publicly traded stock does not mean it cannot be an instrumentality of a foreign government. It is common for many partially privatized companies to have publicly traded shares yet still have substantial state ownership. The mere fact that a company is traded on an exchange can give you no comfort that it is wholly private sector.

Matters are often made murkier because most countries do not have the kind of detailed public disclosure requirements that U.S. companies have. Because of this, you will not be able to vet a company's ownership structure by pulling a 10-K or other similar public document. This fact makes the task of knowing who you are dealing with extremely difficult, and sometimes outright impossible.

This is a big, difficult issue in many developing countries, especially those with a communist tradition (China, Vietnam, and all of the former Soviet republics). But even though you may never have certainty on these issues, you should undertake a due diligence process to know your customers and strategic partners. This diligence process must be clear, uniform, and documented. It is always better to be able to say that you looked for evidence of state ownership in all of the places you could expect to find it and you found nothing than to say it was just too difficult so you never bothered looking at all.

Often this issue can be relatively simple to address, so long as you are willing to implement a process and undertake the administrative burden of following it. This process can begin with simply asking about the ownership structure. Many companies will tell you if they have government ownership (or ownership by individual government officials). When they say they do, you know where you stand. The problem is that just because they say they don't have government ownership doesn't mean they don't. Companies often find themselves in the unfortunate position of trying to prove a negative in circumstances where there is limited information available. But a simple intake form that you ask all of your customers and vendors to fill out is a good start. Having them fill it out again on an annual basis is even better. (Doing this ensures that, if circumstances change, you become aware of them.)

You want to document your efforts. Being able to demonstrate that you have at least some controls in place to ensure you do not violate the FCPA can do a lot for you if anyone ever asks questions after the fact. Remember, the FCPA is all about intent. If you have a process and you are doing the best you can to ensure you are aware of who you do business with, it goes a long way toward undermining any claim that you intentionally violated the law.

And to be clear, I am not saying you cannot do business with state-owned entities or entities owned by foreign officials. What I am saying is that you need to know who you are doing business with because different rules apply to these entities. Some might be tempted to say that the problem is removed if you do not have one set of rules for private entities and another, more conservative set for state-owned entities. If you merely adopt the most conservative policies and procedures, the reasoning goes, you will never have an issue. That may be true, but in my experience, it is highly impractical to do business this way. Many cultures have certain expectations surrounding gifts and entertainment that make a complete restriction on such things far too damaging to implement. These expectations are discussed in detail in the following chapters, but suffice it to say here that you will likely need to know which of your customers or vendors have state ownership.

To illustrate how complex the ownership or control issue can be, let's look at an example drawn from a very well-known case involving the oil services company Baker Hughes. Kazakhstan sits on some of the world's largest oil reserves, and, naturally, the government of Kazakhstan has sought to develop those reserves into producing oil fields. But the process of developing oil fields is extremely expensive. To entice major international oil companies to make long-term investments in the development of those fields, the Kazakhstan government typically grants exclusive rights to develop a particular field to a particular company or, more commonly, a consortium of companies. The consortium and the government typically enter into a production-sharing agreement, which essentially splits the profits from the oil produced in the field between the consortium and the government. The consortium fronts much of the cost of development and recoups those costs from the oil produced. Once the venture starts turning a profit, those profits are split between the government and the consortium. Such was the case in the development of the Karachaganak field in northwestern Kazakhstan.

The consortium with the rights to develop the field was known at the time as KIO but is now known as KPO. KPO is made up of several major international oil companies, and the government of Kazakhstan holds no ownership interest in it. However, as described by U.S. authorities, the Kazakhstan national oil company—then known as Kazakhoil (now known as KazMunaiGaz)—"wielded considerable influence ... and the ultimate award of any contract by the consortium of international oil companies depended upon the favorable recommendation of Kazakhoil officials." (This is the DOJ's description.)

Through a subsidiary, Baker Hughes submitted a bid to provide oil field services on the project. Before the award was announced, Kazakhoil officials demanded that Baker Hughes engage a consulting firm located on the Isle of Man to act as its "agent" in connection with the project. The consulting agreement required payment of a commission equal to 2 percent of the revenue on the current project and 3 percent of the revenues on any future projects. It was undisputed that the consulting firm performed no actual services in connection with the project. In essence, the allegation goes, Baker Hughes agreed to pay a percentage of the contract value into an offshore account and papered the transaction as if it were a payment for a consulting firm. When all was said and done, Baker Hughes and its subsidiary paid a total of $44 million in fines for FCPA violations for this arrangement (which was the largest FCPA fine in history when it was announced in April 2007).

Although the KPO consortium was indisputably private, the U.S. government took the position that its contracting decisions were effectively controlled by the government of Kazakhstan through Kazakhoil's influence. Essentially, Kazakhoil could veto any decision of KPO, and certain Kazakhoil officials used that power to enrich themselves through kickback or bogus commission schemes. The use of third-party consultants and agents receives a much lengthier discussion in Chapter 8, but I hoped that payments to an obviously bogus agent who provides no services whatsoever are transactions that would raise red flags for anyone who is reading this book.

But not all such transactions are as transparent. The point here is that you need to have an understanding of the companies you do business with, especially when you are doing business in an industry that traditionally has a high degree of state control—such as oil or the industries discussed later in this chapter. Often, as with KPO, there is government control over entities (or their decisions) but the entities look and feel *and indeed are* private companies, just as KPO was. This kind of control potentially brings your dealings with those private entities within the purview of the FCPA even though there is no state ownership whatsoever.

Traditionally Controlled Industries

There are numerous cases arising in traditionally state-controlled industries, and I won't go through them all here. The fundamental lesson is that some industries are higher risk than others. Everyone deals with customs, tax, health, safety, environmental, and other regulatory areas, but some industries are, by their very nature, dominated to a large degree by the government, especially in the third world.

We already discussed the oil industry (and there are many other cases besides Baker Hughes). But the same points can be made about the energy and natural resources sectors as a whole. For example, the Portland, Oregon–headquartered Schnitzer Steel was found to have violated the FCPA's anti-bribery provisions for paying kickbacks to managers of state-owned steel mills in China to induce them to purchase scrap metal from Schnitzer. In that case, the SEC brought enforcement actions against both the company and individual executives. One of the executives was alleged to have personally benefited from the scheme in the form of an increased bonus he received as a result of the tainted sales. The total value of the bonus: $15,000. That figure should hold your attention. Bribes do not need to result in multimillion-dollar profits to be actionable. An individual who received a mere $15,000 in benefit was pursued *personally* by the U.S. government.

Mining is another high-risk industry. A recent matter involving British/Australian mining giant Rio Tinto is instructive, both because it demonstrates the state dominance of the natural resources industry and because it reveals the variety of paths allegations can take. In that matter, the Chinese government made allegations that Rio Tinto executives in China bribed certain key executives of some of the nation's 16 state-owned steel mills to obtain allegedly secret information about China's iron ore market. But in an unusual twist, four Rio Tinto executives ultimately pled guilty in China to *receiving* millions of dollars in bribes *from* Chinese officials and stealing secret state information. Rio Tinto's general manager in Shanghai was sentenced to 12 years in prison. The facts of the case are unusual. Apparently Rio Tinto backed out of a deal that would have permitted China's largest diversified mining firm to make a $20 billion investment in the firm. Although the nature of all of the relationships is unclear, the entire saga should serve as a cautionary tale about corruption generally. When you get involved in corrupt relationships, the very officials you pay to be favorable to you can bring the power of the government down on you when you try to back out of an arrangement.

The security and defense industries are another high-risk area. Many of the earliest FCPA cases related to defense contractors, and most would recognize a transaction involving the sale of fighter planes or missiles directly to a foreign government as a high-risk transaction. But many transactions in this area are less obvious.

For example, California-based InVision sold explosive detection systems to airports in Thailand, the Philippines, and China through foreign sales agents. These sales agents sought to influence the airport decision makers with gifts, travel, and payments of cash. Given that airports all over the world commonly are owned or controlled by the government, just as they were in the countries at issue, the decision makers associated with the various airports were all foreign officials under the FCPA.

Telecommunications is another industry fraught with risk since the telecom grids in many developing countries often are owned or controlled by the state. In 2007, Lucent Technologies, which later became part of the French telecommunications company, Alcatel, paid a $2.5 million FCPA fine in connection with its activities in China. In an unrelated case, 20-year Alcatel executive Christian Sapsizian pled guilty in 2008 to violating the FCPA in connection with securing cellular network contracts in Costa Rica. Sapsizian was 62 years old at the time and was sentenced to 30 months in prison, 3 years of supervised release, and forfeiture of more than $260,000. And finally, in early 2010, the merged company, now called Alcatel-Lucent, agreed to $137 million in FCPA settlements with the DOJ and SEC.

Another telecommunications company, California's UTStarcom reached criminal and civil settlements in late 2009 relating to payments made to secure business with state-controlled telecommunications companies in China. The UTStarcom payments are discussed in more detail in Chapter 6, as they are an excellent example of travel and training expenses used to mask illegal bribes. This is an area of particularly high risk when dealing with state-controlled businesses.

Finally, one other industry deserves special note for its high risk, and highly regulated, nature: healthcare. Hospitals and healthcare systems in most countries outside the United States are dominated by foreign governments. In many countries, almost everyone who works at a hospital can be considered a foreign official. Historically, there have been numerous FCPA cases connected to the healthcare industry, from the *Schering-Plough* settlement we discuss in great detail in Chapter 7, to the industry-wide probe into medical device manufacturers that played out throughout 2007 and 2008. The DOJ recognizes the healthcare industry as one of the most attractive industries to focus on, and DOJ officials have gone so far as to announce an intent to engage in an industry-wide examination of the pharmaceutical industry in 2010 and beyond.

One last area worth noting is not industry specific but has to do with international aid programs. These programs often buy a wide variety of goods and services, from food to medicines, to an array of basic and heavy equipment. By their very nature, they are often managed by governmental entities or organizations and generally they are focused on some of the poorest and least stable places in the world. This confluence of factors makes them fertile ground for corruption. There is also a very well-known historical FCPA example: the United Nations Oil-for-Food Programme created for the benefit of the Iraqi people after the 1991 Gulf War.

The kickback arrangements used in the Oil-for-Food schemes typically involved intermediary sales agents in other Middle Eastern countries. The sales themselves were typically at top-flight prices or even at prices above the suggested retail prices sought by the manufacturers. From these prices the sales agents would take a healthy commission and pay a kickback into a bank account in a country outside of Iraq held either in the name of an Iraqi official or by someone connected to the official. In many instances clues should have tipped people off that something was wrong. For example, in some cases, situations arose where a sales agent informed their clients that the relevant Iraqi official demanded a commission in exchange for approving a sale. After being told no commission could be paid, the sales agent might then ask for an increase in *his own* commission that equated to the same percentage previously sought. In many cases, the second request was granted and the sale went through.

These are circumstances that DOJ settlements typically refer to as having a "high probability" of bribery. In these circumstances, even where there is no direct proof of a bribe being paid, the DOJ or SEC will get a settlement or collect a fine on the theory that a company failed to have adequate internal controls to protect against that high probability of bribery. As I've said before, the government doesn't need proof of the bribe to get you.

Businesses Owned by Individual Foreign Officials

The head of the local branch of the tax police, who is in charge of investigating and ultimately enforcing all tax violations in your area, also happens to own the largest local accounting firm. Or, worse, after engaging this local accounting firm (without any knowledge of its ownership), you hear a rumor from your local finance director that the head of the tax police has an "ownership interest" of some kind in the accounting firm. What do you do?

What if it isn't the accounting firm but the security company that guards your warehouses? Does that make a difference? What if the rumor is that it is the head of the tax police's wife who has the ownership interest? His father? Brother? This is a problem all too familiar to anyone who has done business in a smaller city in the third world where certain sectors of the economy often are dominated by specific individuals or families. Sometimes there may be no other option available.

This is one of the toughest FCPA areas to deal with, and it is also one of the most common. It combines the questions of ownership or control with questions about what kind of relationship with a foreign official crosses the line. And it is counterbalanced by the argument that everyone is entitled to make a living and own a business, especially as the degrees of separation open up between the person who owns or controls the business and the government official at issue.

In the scenario just described, if it is the official's brother who owns a security firm, why shouldn't you be able to use it if the rates are reasonable and the service is good? Why should the brother be penalized just because he's related to a tax official? This is a fair argument to make, and, indeed, it is the very one that is made when these facts arise. In fact, many FCPA practitioners might agree that such a scenario might be perfectly legal. But let's unpack these situations and explore the factors that matter most.

At the end of the day, if you do business with a company owned by a foreign official, you need to be able to demonstrate why it is permissible to do so. I walk through various scenarios next in an effort to define the contours of the analysis so you will know what to look for and what questions to ask when this issue arises. I would caution you on making a final judgment call yourself. Involve your legal or compliance department if you can. That may mean delay in making a decision, but trust me, the disruption caused by an FCPA investigation will be much worse.

The main variables in the calculus are these: The closer the relationship to the official and the more relevant the business is to the official's duties, the higher the FCPA risk. The higher the price paid, the higher the risk and the better the quality of the goods or services provided must be. We'll analyze each of these variables next to determine the level of risk associated with them.

The More Relevant the Official to Your Business, the Higher the Risk

Let's start with the relationship to the official. The closest "relationship" is obviously the official him- or herself. Next closest would be the official's spouse. Businesses owned by an official or spouse of an official are high risk. Obviously, any profits from their business are going directly into their pocket. In these cases, the only real question to ask is how relevant the official is to your business. The head of the local tax police owning the accounting firm that does your taxes is a nonstarter. No matter how reasonable the rates, no matter how strong the assurances you get that everything is on the up and up, you will never be able to defend this arrangement if it turns out that your company is getting away with tax violations or otherwise receiving favorable treatment (even with something as seemingly benign as speedy processing of tax refunds). The official has a glaring conflict of interest that you do not want to be connected with.

But what about a father, daughter, or brother owning the accounting firm? As a general matter, these relationships may still be too close for comfort, though other practitioners might go the other way. Certain facts and circumstances might mitigate the risk somewhat, such as being able to demonstrate that your business gets treated just as harshly by the tax authority as other businesses (you still get fined and penalized when you are late or wrong about something). But in my experience these facts seldom exist in such circumstances. More typically, the official's father, daughter, or brother is going to get you speedy processing and minimal or no hassles. Or, at minimum, be able to resolve any disputes "informally" with little or no fines or documentation required. Just as with the official or his or her spouse, this one is hard to defend after the fact when you later learn that you have in fact been getting preferential treatment.

What about a cousin? Practitioners differ on "how close is too close," and this is the line where opinions are all over the map. No one will ever tell you that, as a matter of law, it is legal or illegal to engage an official's cousin to help you in an industry directly within the official's jurisdiction. Other facts will have to be known to make a solid determination. But this is a distant enough relationship that it becomes easier to defend.

Relationships are often difficult to prove. Officials do not come with genealogy charts tattooed on their backs. In many places, rumors of distant or vaguely described relationships abound. The sources are often dubious, and hard information is mercurial at best. Yet you will always be able to find someone who states that "so and so is married to the sister-in-law of official X's cousin." Try running that to ground. The hardest "evidence" of the relationship you'll have may be an off-the-cuff remark by a low-level employee. If that is all you have, you may be able to disregard it if you can show you made an adequate due diligence effort.

What would that diligence effort look like? At minimum, start by asking the alleged "cousin" about the relationship. If the relationship is denied, get a statement in writing to that effect—something to certify the answer to the question and, if possible, make it grounds for immediate termination of your contract if you later learn the representation to be untrue. And document everything. But if the relationship is confirmed, you will need to do more.

How much more depends on what you learn. Often, when you ask the question, the relative will recognize why you are asking and will try to downplay the relationship. You might hear something like: "Sure, Official X is my cousin, but believe me, he doesn't cut me any slack. If anything, we get scrutinized more. The only advantage I have is that he'll always take my phone calls." Can you rely on this? Is the relative just trying to tell you what she thinks you want to hear? These really aren't questions you want to wrestle with, if you can avoid it.

I find it helpful to flip the questions around and ask the business unit manager—perhaps someone not unlike yourself—why you wouldn't just engage another accounting firm. If the answer is a lot of resistance to change coming from the accounting staff, your antennae should go up. Be careful not to lose your objectivity in matters like these. Sometimes, in an effort to back up their own people, I find business unit managers arguing vociferously that a particular supplier or services firm is important because of the history with their business and the relationships they have.

If you are a manager and find yourself making these kinds of arguments, take a step back and ask yourself what is really going on. After all, if you thought you were getting bad advice from your accountant (or your lawyer!), you would change firms in a heartbeat. Why the resistance here? The world is full of service providers.

Usually, resistance to changing firms or suppliers stems from some unstated belief that using the firm with the relationship to the relevant official gives some kind of advantage. Maybe the advantage is only imagined, existing only in the minds of your accounting staff, but don't lose sight of the fundamental fact that the FCPA is about the *intent of the person giving the thing of value.* If your accounting staff believes it gets some advantage, then the decision to give the business to the firm with the relationship to the official may be a problem.

I say *may* because it is certainly not illegal to hire people with good relationships to relevant officials. The lobbying industry in the United States (and around the world) is built around these kinds of personal relationships. It is illegal to offer something to the official with a corrupt motive. Under the facts I just described, there is no evidence that the cousin is doing that. There is not even evidence that your accounting staff believes that the cousin is giving anything of value to the relative to influence him in any way, least of all for your company's benefit. Put in the most positive light, all you have are people on your accounting staff who might believe that, all things being equal, there may be value in using the firm owned by the guy who can at least get phone calls returned when an issue comes up as opposed to a firm owned by someone who has no such access.

Unfortunately, most companies in this situation (and most companies with substantial overseas operations are in this situation, often in many countries, whether they realize it or not) are left in the difficult spot of having to prove a negative. That is, they must prove that the cousin's accounting firm is *not* giving gifts or other things of value to the tax official in an effort to secure an unfair advantage on its behalf. The most conservative approach is to take a hard-line stance and say you simply will not engage consultants who are relatives of relevant government officials. That will deal with this particular problem, but it does not ensure you are free from problems with your consultants and agents.

In Chapter 8 I go into detail about steps you can take with your agents to ensure you have some controls in place to deal with this exact situation. Taking steps on the front end of any consulting or agency relationship to ensure that you can document what an agent can and cannot do on your behalf goes a long way toward proving that you at least thought about these issues and tried to control the risks. A direct relationship with an official is just another of the risks you need to address. It complicates the analysis, but disposing of that single issue does not resolve the complexities of dealing with agents and consultants generally.

The bottom line is that when you are dealing with a third party who has an extremely close familial relationship with a relevant official, you should probably look for other alternatives. Even if you take great pains to ensure the relationship is clean, the risks may be too high and the transaction may be hard to defend if things go bad. Where the relationship is more tenuous, the fact of the relationship can be dealt with in a manner not too different from what you would do with a normal consultant or third-party agent. The relationship is a risk factor you need to be aware of and deal with directly, but it is a risk that can be managed under the right circumstances.

We've been discussing situations where the services at issue are directly related to the official's duties. But perhaps more common is the situation where the related official is in a part of the government that is unrelated to the services provided (or part of the government unrelated to your business). The key question here is whether the official to whom the service provider is connected has any real ability to influence anything of relevance to your business. If the city dog catcher happens to own the accounting firm (and stray animals have no relevance to your business), you're probably all right. But what if it is the spouse of the local health and safety inspector? Or the son of the woman who runs the local immigration office, through which all of your work permits are processed?

The issue here should be obvious: The more relevant the official is to your business, the higher the risk. Where there is no relevance whatsoever, you can probably treat the relationship no different from a relationship with a normal consultant or agent who has no hint of government affiliation. But be careful not to define "relevant" too narrowly. Very senior officials often have very wide influence that transcends their actual job description.

Take the accounting firm example. What if the owner of the accounting firm is the daughter of the country's ambassador to the United States? The ambassador's actual job duties probably have little or no relationship with your business, but could the ambassador help your business? Probably, at least in certain circumstances. Ambassadors are usually well-connected political figures, with direct access to presidential, royal, or parliamentary officials. If you need influence, ambassadors are good people to know. But you would need to be trying to use the relationship in some way for it to be an issue. The mere fact of the relationship itself generally will not be a problem.

I make this point because large multinational companies are vast, and their many parts are not always aware of what every other part is doing. I have seen situations where one business unit within a foreign country is unaware that another business unit is seeking a large contract through senior officials in a ministry or agency in that very same country. In such cases, there may be no one within the organization who can see all of the relationships that may be relevant to the business as a whole.

This is not to say that a pure coincidence of Business Unit A contracting with the ambassador's daughter and Business Unit B lobbying the ambassador to wield some influence on the company's behalf violates the FCPA's anti-bribery provisions. But it does demonstrate how a company puts itself at risk for doing so through lack of internal controls and procedures, which can itself violate the FCPA.

A Note on Payments

So far, I have said nothing about the amount paid for the services. Recall that I started this book dispelling certain rumors persisting around the FCPA. One of these was that there is an exception for payments that are "reasonable." There is no "reasonableness" exception to the FCPA. But that is not to say that the price you pay is irrelevant. Overpaying, or paying market rates for a substandard product, is evidence that the decision to engage a particular consultants or agents may have nothing to do with the services or products they provide. When those agents or consultants are relatives of a foreign official, you have a difficult transaction to defend.

In the end, a rational business never pays more than it has to for goods or services. Similarly, where substandard goods or services are provided, a rational business generally changes providers. Paying too much, or paying market rates for poor service or quality (or paying for goods or services you don't really need at all), indicates that there is some reason to be in the relationship that has nothing to do with the good or services. If the provider is the relative of a foreign official, you will have a hard time finding an innocent explanation for the transaction that will convince government regulators.

CHAPTER 5

Guess Who's Coming to Dinner?
The Dangers of Meals and Entertainment

Taking clients to lunch, dinner, and out for drinks is such a common part of doing business that most managers—even those familiar with the FCPA—are shocked to learn that these practices might constitute a federal crime in certain circumstances. This prospect can be troubling in countries or industries where there are significant state-owned entities and even more so in cultures where meals and drinks are considered a commonplace custom across all business relationships, including those with government regulators and inspectors.

Companies adopt a wide range of strategies for dealing with this problem, and none of them is foolproof. Often it is impractical to have flat prohibitions on meals and entertainment. This is an extreme measure that is unnecessary in most cases, as most businesses have mostly nongovernmental customers. But two policies—one for private commercial companies and another for dealing with governmental and state-owned entity employees—require a sincere commitment to knowing your customers. As we discussed in Chapter 4, that is no easy task in many countries.

In addition, the threshold for what can be considered a "reasonable" expenditure (there goes that concept again; remember that there is no "reasonableness" exception to the

79

FCPA; reasonableness is merely a proxy for intent) changes with each country and even within each country. Just as costs are much higher in Dubai than Jakarta, what passes for fine dining in Shanghai is far more expensive than in Chengdu. It is easy to imagine elaborate, micromanaging grids designed to police very small corporate expenditures in every market around the globe.

Finally, the larger the number of policies and the more complex those policies are, the higher the training and enforcement burden on the company. In companies with a large international presence, the constant training, enforcement, and responses to questions from the field makes compliance with even relatively simple meal and entertainment policies a full-time job.

Wining and Dining Customers

As a practical matter, no one is likely to go to jail because he bought a foreign official a single lobster dinner. But as I mention throughout this book, these events rarely occur in isolation. If you take a step back and think about how business is done with customers generally, what kind of patterns would you expect to see? Here is one that I often see.

The typical pattern is meals and entertainment centered around contract negotiations and awards. I can almost guarantee that when you examine a company's books, you will see a spike in meal and entertainment expenses building up to the negotiation of a major sale or contract award. If you plot the dates and attendees on a calendar, you can almost visualize the negotiation process. An initial meeting or two attended by a couple of key players on both sides, followed by a series of meetings, some with a few attendees, some in much larger groups. Lunches, dinners, drinks, and late-night entertaining. The expenses typically build in frequency and amount until, almost simultaneously with consummation of the deal, they peak and fall off rapidly.

When someone like me takes a team of forensic accountants in to sift through the paper trail left behind, we often are left with serious and difficult questions. Fundamentally, we are trying to sort out whether the reason you won the business was due, at least in part, to the entertaining you did. Did the free flow of expensive meals and nights on the town influence the decision to award you the business? Was that your motivation in taking these people out? Was it at least part of your motivation? If it was not, then why did you do it? These people aren't your friends, after all, and you billed it to the company. What I generally end up with is an inextricably intertwined set of explanations and motivations that may not always point to an FCPA violation but may well point to a lack of controls and a lack of sensitivity to FCPA issues:

> "It's just part of doing business. There's an expectation that you'll all go out after a long day in the conference room. Hell, I can usually make more progress over a couple of scotches than I can in a full day of formal negotiations."
>
> Or, "Look, this was a three-year project. Getting to know each other and making sure they felt comfortable working with us was at least as important as what we were charging, when it came right down to it."
>
> Or, "Of course they're not my friends. It's just cultural. These guys expect to be shown a good time and would be totally offended if we didn't take them out. We wouldn't have gotten a second meeting if we hadn't."
>
> Or, "What's the big deal? We didn't do it all the time, just when the senior guys were there. You have to take them out. It's an embarrassment if you don't, and it puts the guys below them in a tough spot. You don't understand how things are in this country."

These are typical answers I get, and they all point toward a fundamental truth that makes the FCPA especially difficult in certain countries: Business is about personal relationships, and those relationships are not formed in conference rooms. But when you are dealing with foreign officials and employees of state-owned companies, you need to be extra sensitive to the way you go about forming those relationships.

Be Attentive to the Costs

Expenses that seem quite modest by U.S. standards are often considered lavish by local standards. For example, if people are spending $100 a head for dinner with a Chinese government official, you need to pay attention. That is probably half a month's salary for the official. Put in those terms, if you're a manager with a low-six figure salary, imagine if a customer took you out and spent five or six *thousand* dollars a head on "dinner"—what do you think that dinner would be like? Would a dinner like that make an impression on you? What could the purpose of a dinner like that possibly be?

Recall a point I made in the opening chapter regarding the SEC's prohibition on its employees accepting even a sandwich during a lunch meeting. Although the SEC probably has a lot more faith that its personnel would not be influenced by a bad ham sandwich, this policy is aimed at the *appearance* of impropriety. The SEC does not want its employees to ever be in a situation where their motives and integrity can be called into question. You should have the same goals for your employees.

Think about how a dinner at a nice restaurant will look after the fact. Then think about a series of such dinners all clustered around the time of a successful negotiation for your company. Then think about whether your answers to *why* you took the officials to dinner will sound anything like the ones I just set out. While you may scoff at the idea that anyone would make a decision about awarding a large contract because of a few meals, think again about the relative value of those meals. You may be used to nice restaurants and good bottles of wine at business dinners, but the officials you deal with may only rarely, if ever, see the inside of such places (and could never afford them on their own). Perhaps the prospect of a steady flow of such meals and entertainment influenced their decision to give you the business. Wasn't that your intent all along?

This is important for another reason. I have harped on the fact that there is no reasonableness exception to the FCPA. And while it is true that the reasonableness of an expense is at best evidence of a lack of corrupt intent, the unreasonableness of an expense tends to be viewed as much stronger evidence that there *was* corrupt intent. That may not be a fair interpretation, but it is hard to defend lavish spending on foreign officials. The fact of the matter is that all business dinners are motivated, at least in part, by a desire to achieve a good outcome for your company. Otherwise, what is the point? There are certainly examples of business associates with whom you have formed a genuine friendship over the years—people you see socially, completely outside of the work context—but I seriously doubt the foreign officials at issue here fall into that category.

You take them out because you want their business, you want favorable tax treatment, you want to resolve that pesky permitting issue that will allow you to operate legally. All of these are benefits to your business, and all of them will satisfy the "obtain or retain business" or "gain an unfair advantage" requirements of the FCPA. So the only issue left is whether you are acting with a corrupt motive.

You will, of course, say there was no such motive, so your own explanations will be steeply discounted as self-serving. What evidence is left? The pattern of expenses. The amount of the expenses. Questions such as: Should a Chinese government procurement agent who makes 2,000 reminbi a month be eating a 1,000 reminbi dinner at the Jean Georges in Shanghai? Should he be eating there three times in a six-week period?

Those facts have the appearance of impropriety. Make only a single change, and they look very different. Instead of a pattern of meals at nice restaurants, change it to lunches brought into the conference room where the negotiations are taking place. Now your explanation for the expense is: "These were long negotiations, we had to bring lunch in. It was nothing fancy, just basic hospitality. We used the same vendor we always use for the lunches we bring in, even for internal meetings with our own staff."

What is the motive for those meals? To ensure everyone stays focused on the negotiations. The cost? Obviously reasonable and nothing out of the ordinary. Maybe the SEC wouldn't accept the sandwich, but any lawyer would be able to argue pretty aggressively that no one should go to jail simply because a foreign official did.

The Dangers of Entertainment

Pure entertaining—as opposed to a meal—is often higher risk simply because it is harder to claim that there is any business purpose beyond pure relationship building. You can, and probably will, discuss business over a meal. Maybe you will over drinks at the bar or during a round of golf, but you are extremely unlikely to do any meaningful discussion of business during the late-night karaoke session or at the dubious "hostess bar" that doubles as a brothel.

Let's be clear here: In certain cultures, business "entertainment" is very often associated with prostitution. This is the kind of "expense" that is so obviously impermissible that most companies do not even have a written policy that explicitly prohibits it. And to make matters worse, it may be so culturally ingrained that your line sales and marketing people—foreign nationals, raised in the local culture—may not see it as any different from a meal or round of golf, especially if your written policies do not explicitly address it.

In the United States, we are very sensitive to these issues. Employment regulations surrounding sexual harassment and hostile workplace environments make it so some people will not even discuss a topic like this. No one will even acknowledge it. But I would urge you to be explicit with your people to the extent your human resources department will permit it. Tell them in no uncertain terms that paying for prostitutes for clients is never acceptable and that doing so will constitute grounds for automatic termination.

Which takes us to the next topic: fake receipts.

The Problem of the Fake Receipt

I have seen fake receipts in many countries, but China is by far the worst. Most managers—especially those from the United States—do not realize that there is a huge industry in China that supplies fake receipts to anyone who wants them. The general problem with receipts in China is that they are generic in nature. A receipt for a restaurant typically only will indicate that it is from a restaurant and give a total for the expense. No itemized receipt, no way to tell how many people were there or what was ordered. And that's for the *legitimate* receipts.

To make matters worse, it is easy to purchase a receipt that says anything you want it to say, in any amount. The accounting implications are obvious. If every receipt is potentially bogus, how can you (or your auditors) rely on receipts or any other record? This is a serious issue. It is complicated by the fact that many fake expenses are small enough to be approved by low-level personnel and may even be below the testing threshold used by your internal or external auditors when they come through to review the books (if they choose to review these particular accounts at all). But that may be irrelevant in any event, since a fake receipt will look and smell exactly like a real receipt to anyone who does not know exactly what to look for.

The use of fake receipts is so prevalent in China that I have been told on several occasions that low-level inspectors (tax, health and safety, environmental inspectors) actually carry a packet of fake receipts around with them in amounts approximating common bribery amounts (200, 500, 1,000 reminbi) that reflect common types of business expenses (meals, fuel, office supplies). They find a code violation. Your low-level employee wants to make it go away and avoid getting in trouble for failing to do her job. She hands over 500 reminbi. The inspector returns a receipt for nearly the same amount in an expense category through which the employee can get reimbursed easily, and everyone is happy. The low-level employee goes to the accounting department with the receipt and a story about how she had to buy some office supplies, or gas for the truck, or take someone from a legitimate client out to lunch, and promptly gets the cash back.

Or perhaps she offers no story at all. She does not have to. The accounting policy requires all expenses to be supported by a receipt. She has a receipt, so no explanation is necessary, and the accounting staff will ask no questions.

High-Risk Accounting Areas

The problem created by fake receipts is not limited to small expenses. Variations on the outright fraudulent receipt abound. Most of these involve core business functions where the expenses can be high and single vendors are often used to provide a multitude of goods and services. These expense categories, combined with a loose attitude toward documentation, result in ripe and often-used opportunities for slush funds. For the sake of clarity, a slush fund typically refers to a pool of "unaccounted-for" funds that are used for corrupt or illicit purposes.

Here is a typical example. Your company often hosts seminars or conferences at hotels to educate clients and potential clients about your products and to introduce them to your sales and marketing team. Several times a year, or maybe several times a month, the events rotate through various cities and regions. The expenses can be fairly high—renting the banquet room, setting it up, serving coffee, tea, breakfast, lunch, some snacks, having the right audio/visual equipment set up, maybe some breakout rooms. All of it provided by the hotel and billed on a single invoice. Depending on the city and the number of attendees, the costs can vary widely. Maybe $5,000 to $10,000 in a midsize regional city with a small customer base, up to $50,000 or $100,000 in a major market where costs are higher and a lot more people attend.

Expenses like these are very difficult to audit because who's to say that a total bill for $35,000 makes sense but $40,000 does not, especially when all of the line items on the bill appear to be proper expenditures? If a marketing or sales person wanted to free up $5,000 to use for other purposes, this is an easy way to do it, especially in a culture such as China, where many businesses will be very accommodating. Imagine the event coordinator at the hotel agreeing to spread $5,000 extra across the various expense categories in exchange for a $500 kickback out of the $5,000 in cash. The hotel is not out anything. Your company pays the bill with no questions asked. The event coordinator is $500 richer, and your sales or marketing staff has $4,500 to spread around (or pocket). This situation is more common than you think.

Or forget about getting cash. Imagine you have key customers (government or otherwise) attending the conference, and the event planner agrees to make a couple of hotel suites available to them, bring in some women, and provide whatever they ask for from room service (liquor, food, a tailored suit, jewelry from the gift shop in the lobby). The costs are again spread around the other legitimate expense categories on the invoice with a little "service fee" tacked on for the event planner's trouble. And you will almost never be able to spot it.

Just to ratchet up your paranoia, imagine this: A conference that never happened at all. I've seen it, and it isn't pretty. A multipage invoice from a hotel that includes all of the routine expenses associated with a conference, but the accounting records do not reflect any purchases of plane tickets for the sales staff to fly to the city to attend the conference. No one has any PowerPoints or attendee lists or any of the other materials they should have for a conference that really happened. Indeed, travel records for key employees who should have attended show them in different cities on the day of the seminar. The employees who allegedly attended give markedly different descriptions of who attended, what was discussed, how many people were there, even whether lunch was served or not. Eventually, some employees start saying things like "I go to lots of conferences. Maybe I didn't actually go to this one, I just can't remember." And eventually, under heavy questioning, someone cracks. There was no conference. "My boss told me what to say. I have no idea where the money went."

Two other areas where this kind of problem is common are travel expenses and event sponsorships. Travel agencies typically do high-volume business with companies, an arrangement where it is easy to hide excess costs or spread them around. Imagine instances where the travel agent arranges an entire travel package, including hotel expenses. Now there are two layers of invoices where expenses can be hidden and cash funneled out. (After all, your travel agent can play the same games with the hotel invoice I described as well as similar games with its own invoice.) If the travel agency is cooperative—and in many developing countries they certainly can be—anything you want can be buried in the invoices as long as the overall bill is not so outrageous that it is unbelievable on its face.

Event sponsorships, typically associated with conventions, industry groups, or trade association activities, are also fertile grounds for slush funds because these are typically single-line-item invoices for fairly large amounts. Your company is going to be a premier-level sponsor of a trade show—the fee is $50,000, and you get a premium booth location and signage all over the convention center. Where does that $50,000 go? Ostensibly toward the cost of the convention, but again, maybe only $40,000 or $45,000 goes there and $5,000 goes back to your sales department so it has money to entertain clients who come to the convention.

One final problem area that I am starting to see more and more is the use of virtual corporate credit cards, commonly referred to as p-cards (procurement cards) or ghost cards. Any CPAs out there will excoriate me for failing to spell out the distinctions between the two (technically, they are different), but for our purposes here, they are essentially the same thing. Depending on how they are set up, they give certain company employees the ability to charge expenses at particular vendors, or expenses at a particular category of vendors, without the need for a physical credit card. Those expenses are then charged back to their appropriate accounts on a fairly automated basis.

Accounts payable departments love these cards because it streamlines their jobs. (They no longer have to individually process and pay dozens, or hundreds, of invoices from the same vendor for the same category of expenses each month.) This obviously reduces administrative costs, but it also increases risk. Individual expenses are no longer subject to the same level of scrutiny they would be if they were individually processed and paid. The entire system rests on the assumption (perhaps faulty) that any expenses incurred at a particular vendor are in fact legitimate business expenses. It also assumes that the vendors themselves would never engage in the kind of false invoicing practices discussed earlier. Where either (or both) assumption is false, you have a compliance nightmare.

Needless to say, these assumptions can easily be wrong in high-corruption countries, even if the vendor at issue is generally well known and reputable. Imagine a prominent hotel chain that has locations in many of the places you do business that has agreed to provide good corporate discounts in exchange for being able to bill directly and get guaranteed payment. Just because the chain is well known and reputable in the United States is no assurance that the standards of propriety are the same everywhere.

This is the kind of discussion that causes managers to throw up their hands and tell me I am crazy. They say, "How can I manage a business if I have to second guess everything that goes on?" Or, "I have to be able to rely on and trust the people who work for me." Both are very fair statements.

The point of this discussion is not to grind your operations to a standstill through paranoia and mistrust. The point is only to make you aware that these things are common enough that you need to be concerned about them and vigilant against them. This is where setting the right tone is important. Make sure your employees understand that *you* understand how these transactions work and that they are flat-out prohibited.

Then pay attention. Do certain costs seem high? Ask questions about what exactly the sponsorship fee is for. Try to arrange to show up at sales conferences and seminars unannounced. Make sure your people are aware that you are paying attention.

The truth is that an employee who is determined to circumvent your policies and engage in these activities is probably going to be able to get away with it, at least for a while. You want to make sure that any such employee will appear to be a rogue who is operating outside your clearly defined practices. This protects the company by showing that it is doing everything it can to make sure honest employees do business the right way. It also protects you, because you will be able to show that you have talked about these issues, sent a clear message, taken steps to check up on people, and made sure they follow the rules.

CHAPTER 6

Ensuring That Business Trips Really Are for Business

L ike meals and entertainment, taking clients—especially high-value ones—on trips to play golf, see the sights, and maybe conduct a little business is common. And just like meals and entertainment, such trips can violate the FCPA.

In its least nuanced form, there is a basic assumption that a company—especially a publicly traded company whose assets are ultimately owned by its public shareholders—has an obligation to use corporate assets only for the benefit of the corporation. To that end, just as with meals and entertainment, any use of corporate funds to pay for travel should be for a business purpose. If an employee expends corporate funds for travel (or anything else) of a purely personal nature, that is embezzlement. But just because an expense is not personal does not mean it is a legitimate business expense. After all, a bribe is not personal but clearly is intended to benefit the business.

To be sure, there are legitimate reasons to pay for the travel costs of government officials or employees of state-owned entities. It is also true that merely sending an official on an all-expense paid vacation does not, in and of itself, violate the FCPA. As I have said throughout this book, the focus is on the intent of the person paying. Is there a corrupt motive behind the trip?

Is the intent of the trip to curry favor with an official who can help your business in some way? Are you hoping the official will exercise discretion in a way that is beneficial for your company? Because corporate expenses must be for the benefit of the corporation, the answer to these questions will generally be yes. Otherwise, why would the company be paying for them?

But this does not mean that every corporate expenditure on travel for foreign officials is an automatic FCPA violation. The FCPA contains an affirmative defense to its anti-bribery provisions if:

> *the payment, gift, offer, or promise of anything of value that was made, was a reasonable and bona fide expenditure, such as travel and lodging expenses ... directly related to—*
>
> **A.** *the promotion, demonstration, or explanation of products or services; or*
> **B.** *the execution or performance of a contract with a foreign government or agency thereof.*[1]

This affirmative defense is commonly referred to as the "promotional expense exception," which is a misleading description. An "exception" would be activity the statute explicitly says is *not* a violation. That is, it is activity that falls outside the parameters of the statute. For example, the much-misunderstood facilitating payments exception is in fact an exception. The FCPA explicitly states that it "shall not apply to any facilitating or expediting payment." If it is a facilitating payment, it simply is not covered by the FCPA.

An affirmative defense is a completely different animal. An affirmative defense is essentially a violation that is permitted by

---

[1]See Appendix 1, Sec. 78dd-1(c)(2).

the statute because of the existence of some additional facts that make the violation permissible. But to assert an affirmative defense, the accused must admit that the conduct occurred. Where an affirmative defense applies, the practical outcome may well be the same for a defendant as an exception—no criminal conviction—but the distinction matters.

While this may sound like hypertechnical legalese, the distinction between an exception and an affirmative defense reflects an important substantive perspective that should not be glossed over. I often hear people say "Promotional expenses are permissible"—which is true, under the right circumstances—but that is not the same as saying promotional expenses cannot violate the FCPA. When you assert an affirmative defense, you are admitting to all of the activities that violate the statute, plus asserting additional facts—here, the promotional nature of the expense—that absolve you of liability. But if for any reason there is a problem with the additional facts and the U.S. government—or a jury—doesn't accept them, guess what? You've just *admitted* to an FCPA violation. Thus, the better way to think about it is to say that promotional expenses *are violations* of the FCPA that the statute permits under the right circumstances.

This affirmative defense is essentially a nod to practical business reality. Without the affirmative defense, the FCPA would bar almost every activity that would allow U.S. companies to be competitive in the global market. I discuss the promotional expense defense here because it most often arises in connection with travel expenses for government officials. Here are some of the common scenarios:

- Your products are highly regulated. To enter a new market in a certain country, you need to demonstrate that your manufacturing process complies with the regulatory requirements in place in that country. The only practical way to do this is to bring the government inspectors to your factory in the United States so they can inspect it and certify that the factory complies with their regulations.

- To carry out a large project in a certain country, you will need to import a substantial piece of expensive and highly technical equipment into the country. The equipment cannot be certified for use in the foreign country until it passes the proper inspections. Because the equipment is difficult and expensive to move and set up, it is highly beneficial to have a preliminary inspection conducted before it is shipped so that any obvious defects can be identified and remedied while it is still in its home location and much more easily modified or repaired. The only way to conduct that preliminary inspection is to bring the relevant officials to wherever the equipment is located.

- Your world sales meeting, which is generally only for internal personnel, will be held at a famous U.S. resort. All of your most high-level personnel will be there, including technical experts and others needed to ensure your global sales force has all of the latest information on your newest products. At the same time, you are engaged in a pitch to sell some of your newest products to a major state-owned company in a certain country. Because it is virtually impossible to have all of your best people in the same place at the same time, it is beneficial to bring the relevant officials from the state-owned company to the sales conference where they can be given a half-day demonstration of the products by your best people.

In each of these cases, you are providing something of value to the foreign officials in the form of travel to the United States. In each case, you are hoping to obtain or retain business through the inspection, demonstration, or certification of your products or equipment. Described this way, each of these activities sounds like a violation. Indeed, the only real question for liability purposes is whether the offer of travel is made for a corrupt purpose. Are you attempting to influence the official's discretion by providing what will likely look and feel like exotic travel to a poorly paid foreign official who otherwise might never be able to afford foreign travel of any kind?

Viewed from the perspective of what constitutes a proper business expense, the purpose of this kind of travel will almost always be, in part, an effort to get a favorable decision from the foreign official. The promotional expense affirmative defense recognizes this inherent problem. There are legitimate business needs in each of the scenarios described (e.g., you really cannot get the needed factory certification without the factory inspection), but in each case, that legitimate motive is also mixed with the potentially corrupt motive to secure a favorable decision. The affirmative defense essentially permits a company to move forward with certain expenses where this mixed motive problem exists—but only where a genuine and legitimate business purpose exists, and only where the expenses incurred relate solely (or almost solely) to that purpose.

Ensuring a Proper Business Purpose

The promotional expenses affirmative defense cannot be used as a ruse to pay for elaborate travel that is only tangentially related to a legitimate business purpose. FCPA practitioners differ on how much incidental nonbusiness travel is permissible in connection with a legitimate business trip, but all practitioners generally agree that it must be *incidental*. That is, only a small portion—if any—of the travel can be unrelated to the business purpose.

To take an extreme example—which I have actually come across in my practice—you cannot take state-owned customers on a two-week tour of European capitals, staying at all of the best hotels and eating at the best restaurants, simply so you can execute a major sales contract on the last day of the tour. There is no reason the contract signing cannot occur in your office (or the official's office) back in the relevant country. The travel has no relationship whatsoever to the purported business purpose. Indeed, the only purpose such travel could have is to curry favor with the officials so they will actually *want* to sign the contract. If you've read this far, you already know better than to try this.

But let's use the more common example of the world meeting at the fancy resort, set out earlier. You want to fly in some key decision makers from a state-owned potential customer so that they can receive a half-day presentation by your very best sales and technical experts. If the world meeting is at Hilton Head, can you take the officials out for a round of golf after the presentation? Perhaps they have to stay overnight at the resort because there are no flights out until the following day, and the golf outing was already planned. If the meeting is at the Ritz Carlton in Laguna Beach, can you take the officials to Disneyland? If it is in Sedona, can you arrange a helicopter tour of the Grand Canyon?

Take any of the other scenarios described. Can you fly the officials first class? Can you put them up in a suite? Can you take them out to dinner at all, and if so, how fancy can the meal be? These may feel like petty questions, but they present real, practical difficulties that businesspeople may not even think about until they find themselves in an awkward social situation, where the pressures might cause them to err on the side of including the officials in an activity rather than risk social embarrassment (thereby undermining the entire purpose for the trip).

There are a couple of general rules that can help weed out some of the problems. Overall, you want to remove as much obviously nonbusiness activity from the itinerary as you can. First, try to schedule the meetings with the officials in a way that avoids awkward social situations. Try not to have the meeting in the morning before everyone else is going off to the usual afternoon of planned activities, such as sightseeing or golf. Odds are someone will feel pressure to invite the officials. (After all, what is the big deal, it was already planned and you are only inviting a few extra people.)

These events clearly have a legitimate business purpose, but that purpose is entirely separate from the reason why the officials are there. You have activities at your meetings to foster team building and to ensure that your own people get to know each other and get comfortable with one another. Including potential customers in those activities runs counter to that purpose and changes the entire dynamic. I generally advise that the officials be at the event (or the factory or the corporate headquarters) for the shortest time possible to limit these risks. If there is a half-day of legitimate meetings and a half-day of social activities, it becomes difficult to argue that the social activities were incidental to the business purpose. After all, who's to say the business meeting wasn't incidental to the planned social activities? When they're of equal weight on the itinerary, it becomes difficult to defend.

Indeed, the DOJ has formally opined on this exact subject, but the circumstances are not helpful other than to make the point that entertainment that is truly incidental to the business purpose is permissible. In September 2007, the DOJ approved a proposal by an anonymous company (which is typically how DOJ opinions are issued) to bring six "junior to mid-level officials of a foreign government" who were already in the United States to its headquarters for a five-day training session. In connection with the five-day stay, the DOJ approved "a modest four-hour city sightseeing tour" for the officials. To be clear, the ratio of four hours of entertainment to five days of training is not a mandated ratio (DOJ opinions do not set binding precedent), but this should give you a sense of what I mean by "incidental."

Second, to the extent possible, let the foreign government select the attendees. This always establishes a good fact because your company will not look like it is targeting any particular officials. Whoever the foreign government designates as the appropriate attendee, that is who comes. There may be many circumstances where there is only one logical official to send, in which case this fact will be of less value. But even in those cases, it is helpful to ask the foreign government to select the attendee. At minimum, your request will clearly document that you were being transparent in extending the offer.

Third, regardless of the situation, never treat the officials any better than you treat your own people. If your foreign managers are flying coach to the meeting, make the officials fly that way too. (Indeed, I generally advise making the officials fly coach even if you do fly your own people business class.) Put the officials in the same kind of room everyone else gets. Feed them the same food everyone else eats. Ferry them to and from the airport the same way as everyone else—do not rent them a stretch limo when rank-and-file employees just take cabs.

But even this rule needs to be tempered by common sense. At your world meeting, you very well might have a few upscale events or meals planned that might not be appropriate for the foreign officials to attend even though they would be treated the same as everyone else at the event. The way I look at it is that any event that would be viewed by rank-and-file employees as a real perk—something much nicer than the standard run-of-the-mill business fare—should not be made available to foreign officials. In other words, it is one thing to say the officials got treated the same as everyone else when what is at issue is the standard chicken dinner served at a nondescript corporate banquet; it is quite another to say they were treated just like everyone else, when the "everyone else" is the CEO and a select group of top executives dining at an exclusive Michelin-starred restaurant. The first is incidental to the business purpose of having the officials there to promote your products. The second may fall into the wining-and-dining category discussed in Chapter 5.

When determining what is sufficiently incidental to the primary business purpose, a countervailing principal deserves recognition: Foreign officials are still people entitled to basic courtesy and respect. The mere fact that they are foreign officials does not mean that they must be treated poorly. They do not have to sleep in the supply closet and subsist on bread and water. The trick is to achieve a commonsense balance. The business purpose must be real and legitimate, and the expenses must be of a kind and quality that is above reproach and easily justified as related to the business purpose. This is vague guidance, I realize, but the FCPA literature does set out some clear examples of what is not permissible, which are discussed next.

Ensuring the Expenses Are Related to the Business Purpose

Accounting for the myriad expenses incurred on a business trip can be a hassle. One solution is to pay a per diem that is calculated to approximate the likely expenses, given the location. I generally advise against paying a per diem of any kind to foreign officials. Any time you are simply handing cash to an official, you open yourself up to scrutiny. Even if you pay your own employees a per diem to attend certain events, my view is that the administrative convenience of doing so with foreign officials is far outweighed by the risk it creates. If you are truly paying the expenses of so many foreign officials that your accounting department is simply overwhelmed trying to track them all, I would suggest that is a red flag in and of itself.

Per diems have a fundamental problem in that they are only an *estimate* of likely costs and, by definition, are open to the suggestion that they are too high and allow the recipient to pocket the unused cash. The most famous case involving per diems establishes what should be an obviously inappropriate use. In the well-known *Metcalf and Edy* case from 1999, the company estimated a per diem and then paid the official 150 percent of the per diem as well as first-class travel for the official and his wife and kids.

It is difficult to make the case that paying the travel expenses for spouses and children ever qualifies as a proper business expense. But it should go without saying that estimating the likely travel costs and then paying the official 150 percent of that estimate is tantamount to admitting that you are deliberately putting excess cash into the official's pocket.

But while *Metcalf and Edy* illustrates one extreme example, every use of a per diem is open to criticism or after-the-fact questions. How was the estimate calculated? Who's to say what is an appropriate level of expense? If a per diem is used, will the company really be in a position to prove that it did not also directly pay for any of the official's costs (because that is the whole point of the per diem, right?), thereby leaving the official free to pocket the per diem? These are the kind of needless questions that I generally advise clients to avoid by avoiding per diems.

When paying the travel expenses of foreign officials, pay as many of the expenses directly to the vendors as possible. This can be logistically difficult, but it avoids having to explain and justify the payment of cash directly to an official.

Surely you can arrange to pay for plane tickets and hotels directly through your travel agent. You will likely have the official met at the airport, and the official will probably be accompanied just about everywhere when not in the hotel room. Have a company employee pay for any expenses directly and then get reimbursed for them. That way you will have proper supporting documentation, in addition to a company employee who can attest to being present and being certain that nothing else was provided to the official.

The Government Really Does Bring These Cases

For many years, *Metcalf and Edy* was the only case that spoke directly to travel costs as a basis for FCPA violations. In that matter, it was obvious that excess funds were being given to the official and his family without any plausible connection between the costs and any legitimate business purpose. Because of its extreme nature, *Metcalf and Edy* did not provide much guidance.

In recent years, when companies have gotten in trouble over a variety of FCPA problems, we see mentions of improper travel recited as one of a litany of issues clustered around some larger improper behavior (e.g., the securing of a contract or sale). The aforementioned *InVision* matter is one example. In the SEC's cease-and-desist order against InVision, which centered on sales of explosive detection devices for use in airports, the SEC stated that InVision's Chinese sales agent "intended to offer foreign travel and other benefits to airport officials" in an effort to avoid certain financial penalties associated with the sales.

But cases like these, which typically involve other transactions that are regarded as "core" FCPA areas—the securing of contracts or sales—left open the question of whether U.S. enforcement authorities would pursue a case against a company where the only (or at least a substantial majority of) FCPA issues were travel related. That question was resolved in the affirmative with the case against telecommunications equipment maker UTStarcom Incorporated.

To be clear, the UTStarcom matter involved more than just providing travel to foreign officials, but travel was a major focus of the matter, which, overall, rested on the kinds of wining and dining expenses we have discussed here and in Chapter 5.

Indeed, it is a very good example of the common techniques used to funnel benefits to officials in ways that are difficult for the untrained eye to spot. As we discuss in Chapter 7 and in the chapter on consultants, UTStarcom employed strategies such as providing jobs to relatives of foreign officials, providing lavish gifts and entertainment, in addition to substantial foreign travel.

UTStarcom sold wireless network equipment to many major Chinese cities. Its customers were government-controlled telecommunications companies. The standard installation contract included a provision requiring UTStarcom to pay for some of its customers' employees to attend overseas training sessions at UTStarcom facilities. After each installation was complete, UTStarcom would direct the customers to contact a particular travel agent and choose a destination for the trip. The SEC's complaint states that:

> *Between 2002 and 2007, [UTStarcom] spent nearly $7 million on approximately 225 trips for customer employees pursuant to training provisions in systems contracts.*

* * *

> *Very little documentation was maintained relating to the trips, and [UTStarcom] did not have adequate internal controls to determine whether the trips were in fact for training purposes. On many of the trips, no training actually occurred. Instead, customer employees visited popular tourist destinations where [UTStarcom] had no facilities.*[2]

This summary is interesting. In just a few sentences it refers to a whole range of different travel-related issues. It first focuses

---

[2]For the full SEC complaint, visit: www.sec.gov/litigation/complaints/2009/comp21357.pdf.

on the basic internal controls and record-keeping problems that are easy to imagine. With 225 trips, most of which presumably involved numerous officials, spread over a five-year period, it was probably impossible to say, after the fact, which trips included training sessions. With company turnover and without keeping strict records of every presentation, including the PowerPoints used and the sign-in sheets reflecting the attendance, who could ever say what specific training—if any— occurred on a particular trip? That problem alone would be the basis for an FCPA books and records case if it was clear that foreign officials went on some of the trips.

Also, the summary notes that many trips involved no training whatsoever (implicit in this finding then is that some trips did involve training, but the records were so poorly kept that no one could sort out which were which). It also states that some of the trips went to locations where UTStarcom had no facilities. The implication is that such trips must have been problematic, although it is not clear why. Certainly quality training can occur somewhere other than a location where UTStarcom had a facility. But the contracts apparently specified that the training would be held in locations where the company had facilities.

Which makes a point I try to emphasize to clients all the time: Be careful what you put in your contracts. Language that may sound good on the front end ("We'll have the trainings where we have facilities, how could anyone ever question that?") becomes a source of liability if you later fail to comply with your own contractual requirements. What if you later decide it is more convenient to hold a large training at a hotel somewhere?

The takeaway should be clear. You can pay for travel if there is a legitimate and provable business purpose, but you should assume it will be subject to heavy scrutiny after the fact. The FCPA assumes that most such expenses are incurred for the purpose of influencing the relevant official but provides an affirmative defense for legitimate promotional activities. But the expenses must be carefully tailored to the actual promotional needs. Anything provided beyond what is necessary to conduct the promotional activity can at most be only incidental to the business purpose. As I have said many times already, this is a tricky area and the minutiae are important. Keep meticulous records. Raise the issue to the right people in your company, and let them make the final call.

CHAPTER 7

Gifts That Give Back

After the last two chapters, it will not surprise you that gifts other than meals and travel cause FCPA problems, too. Gifts are unique, however, because many cultures have certain gift-giving expectations that can cause serious compliance problems. As a manager, you may be told that it is local custom to give this or that during certain festivals or holidays. You may be told by your sales staff that their relationships with customers will be damaged if they do not give the expected gifts. Failure to give gifts will be offensive. All of your competitors give them, they will say. Your company will look bad if it gives nothing. And the proposed gift giving will not run solely to customers (and state-owned entities) but also to foreign officials with whom you deal on regulatory matters on a regular basis.

But before we get into the very difficult area of what I call "maintaining your relationships" with foreign officials, we should check off a few of the more obvious categories of prohibited gifts. Gifts of anything that is actually valuable should be avoided. Golf club memberships (or golf clubs), Swiss watches, jewelry, electronics, and anything else of value that anyone would consider a nice gift should be avoided. In contrast, items of truly minimal value are not problematic: pens, baseball caps with the company logo on them, and the usual assortment of low-value promotional items that companies everywhere hand out and that most people might use but do not really want.

As a general matter, many practitioners consider gifts with company logos on them to be within the scope of the afore-mentioned promotional expense defense. But I always caution people not to get too cute. It is easy if we are talking about giving someone a shirt with the company logo—the same shirt the company gives out to its own employees and all of its regular customers. But merely placing a company logo on a gift does not automatically transform it into an acceptable gift. Having the company logo put on the back of a Rolex does not suddenly make it all right to hand out Rolex watches to foreign officials. A truly expensive gift is impermissible and cannot be cleansed of its prohibited nature through the application of a company logo.

Another, less obvious, problem is the use of company assets that are often made available to good customers. Use of a company-owned condo at a ski or beach resort or use of company planes, boats, and cars should be avoided or, at a minimum, heavily vetted by people with a very sophisticated understanding of the FCPA. I hear some practitioners say that use of these items can be cured by charging the official proper rental rates for the items in question—the nightly rental of the condo or the equivalent of first-class airfare for the use of the private plane.

But this cure has always felt unsatisfying to me, and I am not certain companies really want to get into valuation games involving certain assets. For example, is flying on a private jet *really* the same value as first-class airfare on a regular carrier? Most people would probably say it is much more valuable. But there is a more fundamental problem in that companies generally are not equipped to suddenly enter the equipment rental market when a foreign official becomes involved. They do not know the rental value for such things, and they have no real mechanism in place for actually accepting money from an official. To say nothing of the total awkwardness of standing on the deck of your company's ski lodge and accepting cash or a check from an official with whom you are trying to build a relationship. I generally advise companies to stay away from these situations. If officials want to go on vacation, what is so special about your boat or condo? They can rent another. The world is full of them.

The real-world situations where these issues arise are not necessarily as obvious as you might think. Rarely does an official come to you and say, "Hey, I'm looking for a place in Jackson Hole, do you guys happen to have one? What's the rate?" And, while most people with any sense can see that simply making the company plane available to a foreign official to take him and his family wherever he might like to go is a problem, real-life situations are rarely that obvious.

Imagine that the company plane is taking several executives to an industry conference and there happens to be an empty seat. The seat is going whether someone sits in it or not. It costs the company nothing to make the seat available to an official from the same city who is also attending the conference, yet the seat is very valuable to the official. Can you give it to her? This is a hard question that requires a whole range of specific considerations that only an expert can resolve. (And the answer will depend on the specific facts of each situation, facts that you might not even think to consider, such as whether the official is relevant to some other portion of the business completely unrelated to the work that you do.)

Another area to watch is the provision of free samples of your products. It might be fairly obvious if you work for diamond mining company that you should not go around handing out samples of your diamonds to foreign officials. But it may be less obvious if you sell obscure industrial materials that have no practical use to the common man, unless they happen to participate in your industry and have a direct use for the materials. But this is precisely the kind of example that is the most dangerous.

As we discussed in Chapter 4 on state-owned entities, many relatives of officials own businesses that may participate in your industry. Free samples given to the right party can be highly valuable.

Furthermore, free samples are very common in many industries as a method of discounting the sales price between private parties while maintaining a much higher public list price (to throw competitors off). As a matter of routine, your company may have a sales force that has authority to give "discounts" of up to 10 percent, 15 percent, or whatever percent off the list price, but the discount is given in the form of free goods or samples. In the case where you are dealing with a state-owned entity or an entity owned by a relative of an important official, these free goods or samples can have a much more troubling appearance. It may only be a standard discount given in the normal course of your business, but in the case of business with state-owned entities or foreign official ownership, your records will need to be rock solid on that point to avoid any difficult questions after the fact.

"Maintaining" Your Relationship with the Government

Cultural festivals in many countries—especially in Asia—traditionally involve gift giving. Businesses often dole out many low-value traditional gifts to their good customers and potential customers. If you find yourself managing a business in such a country, be sure to understand to whom the gifts are being given and exactly what the gifts are.

If your organization is large, you may find yourself approving a budget and leaving it up to your staff to decide who gets what. This is a dangerous prospect. When you do this, you effectively create a miniature slush fund, the sole purpose of which is to give gifts and over which there is essentially no oversight.

Demand specifics. Exactly who will receive gifts, and exactly what will the gifts be? The more detail the better, because you will be surprised what your staff might do, especially if you lack the cultural experience to spot a problem area.

Let's take a common one: mooncakes given for the Autumn Festival in China. Mooncakes are small cakes made with lotus root that come in various flavors and sizes. They also come in a range of prices. You may be told that all your salespeople have selected their top 20 customers, and marketing has identified another 50 potential customers, so that all in you plan to give mooncakes to 250 recipients. You will then be presented with a budget of 75,000 reminbi (about $10,000). You do the math in your head—about $40 per customer—ask a few questions about why this is necessary ("We'll look bad if we don't do it, we'll offend our customers, everyone expects gifts during the festival, and this is the most culturally traditional gift of all") and you'll say fine and never think about it again. In doing so, you have made several assumptions that are reasonable from your point of view but that may be completely wrong.

First, you probably assume that the equivalent of $40 is an appropriate price for mooncakes. After all, a holiday gift valued at $40 is no big deal by U.S. standards. You would be wrong. Sure you can spend that much on mooncakes, but they are going to be awfully nice ones.

Second, you probably assumed that everyone is getting the same thing. I should note here that the mooncake is analogous to the Christmas fruitcake in the West. Sure, it's a traditional gift, but few people actually like them or want them (let alone want to receive a flood of them from all of their customers). The fact of the matter is that you can buy perfectly acceptable mooncakes for $10, give those out to 240 people on the list, and then have $7,600 left in your miniature slush fund to give something much nicer to your 10 most important people (some or all of whom may be government officials).

This leads to your third assumption: that mooncakes actually are being given. This may be totally incorrect, or correct only in the most technical sense. One common scenario is the mooncake being used as a trafficking device for something much more valuable—for example, a $4,000 "mooncake" that comes with a Cartier watch wrapped around it. Again, you'll have a receipt from a shop that says you bought mooncakes, and with our slush fund example, you would have plenty of cash available to slip one or two of these into the pile. Mooncakes can be packaged with anything from jewelry to electronics—imagine a mooncake that comes with a string of pearls or a plasma television—and vendors in China cater to this kind of gift giving.

Finally, there is the problem of the cash-equivalent coupon. Think about the logistics of actually delivering all of the gifts. It is a big pile of stuff to carry around. It would be a lot easier if the gifts came in an envelope that could be dropped off in person on a regular sales call or simply dropped in the mail along with a holiday card (at least in countries with decent mail service). Enter the gift card. Now, instead of using the budget to purchase physical mooncakes (or whatever the item is in whichever country), the budget purchases gift cards or coupons in various denominations. The problem with these coupons is that in many countries, they are redeemable for cash. The vendor may take a small cut for effectively acting like a bank, but the recipients get money in their pocket rather than mooncakes in hand. If you have government officials or employees of state-owned entities on your list, you have effectively handed them a wad of cash masked as a traditional holiday gift. The problems this creates should be obvious by now.

Cash gifts have a long historical tradition, especially in China and Korea. They may no longer be given in their traditional red envelope packaging, but they remain very much a part of traditional business in those countries. While it may seem unimaginable to an American to get up at a business dinner and walk around the table handing out envelopes full of cash to your guests, this is in fact what happens. Gift cards are just another form of the same thing and are much easier to account for in the company's books.

Efforts to conduct business this "old" or "traditional" way occasionally can have comical results. I once heard a story about a fairly low-level employee in charge of preparing the red envelopes and handing them out at a dinner to be attended by several senior officials who had jurisdiction over a plant that needed final approval from their agencies before operations could commence. The only person he knew at the dinner was his own boss, who had directed him to prepare the envelopes. He arrived slightly late to the dinner, having thought ahead to prepare several extra envelopes just in case someone brought a guest. It turned out that also present at the dinner was the company's regional manager, whom the low-level employee had never met. When the time came to pass around the envelopes, the nervous young employee made his way around the table shaking each person's hand and slipping each attendee an envelope. When asked why he gave an envelope full of the company's cash to his own regional manager, the employee replied: "Look, I didn't know anyone at the table. My job was to pass out the envelopes, so that's what I did." Still tougher to explain was why the regional manager kept his envelope and never said anything to anyone.

Gifts are common fodder in FCPA cases, and many of the best-known cases include references to gifts. As I have asked rhetorically before, what could the purpose of giving corporate gifts possibly be if not to benefit the company in some way? That is certainly the view taken by U.S. enforcement authorities. And to be sure, the gifts need not be high-value to catch the U.S. government's attention.

In 2010, the SEC settled an enforcement action with California-based Veraz Networks, Inc. arising from gifts to state-owned telecommunications clients made by the company's agent in China and its reseller in Singapore. The Chinese agent offered gifts valued at $4,500 and a "consulting fee" valued at $35,000, to employees of a state-owned potential customer. Separately, Veraz's reseller in Singapore offered unspecified gifts and entertainment (including a specifically mentioned gift of flowers) to the CEO and wife of the CEO of a state-owned Vietnamese telecommunications company. Altogether, the total amount of documented gifts was approximately $40,000, for which Veraz paid a $300,000 fine. And this is not the only case where something small and relatively petty gets explicit mention in a settlement.

When Avery Dennison settled its FCPA matter with the SEC, the SEC settlement documents contained a reference to a single gift of shoes to four foreign officials valued at approximately $125 per official. So if you think small amounts cannot land you in trouble, think again. Using gifts to "maintain" or improve your relationships with foreign officials is a high-risk endeavor, and even low-value gifts can look bad in the cold light of hindsight.

Donations

Donations are a particular kind of gift worthy of scrutiny mainly because of the well-known matter of *Schering-Plough*. The *Schering-Plough* case is worthy of some detailed discussion, not only for the donations issue itself but also because of what it says about the FCPA's record-keeping requirements and the aggressive view the U.S. government takes of them.

Schering-Plough Corporation was one of the world's best-known pharmaceutical companies, with operations all over the world. In 2004, Schering-Plough settled an FCPA matter with the SEC based on activities of the Polish branch of one of its Swiss subsidiaries. According to the settlement, the Polish branch donated approximately $76,000 over a two-year period to a charitable foundation established to restore castles and historic sites in Poland. There was no dispute that the charity was a real, bona fide, and legitimate one. This is not a case involving a sham entity that did none of what it purported to do. The charity was really out there restoring castles and other historical sites. Furthermore, there was no dispute that the donations the Polish branch made went into the charity's coffers and were used for those purposes. This was also not a case of the charity masking as a front for direct payments of cash to a foreign official. There was no allegation that an official was simply taking the cash out the back door of the charity, and certainly no allegation that the Polish branch made the donations knowing an official would do so.

At issue was the fact that the founder of the charity was also the director of a regional government body in Poland that either directly purchased or could influence the purchase of pharmaceuticals. Although the quantity of donations Schering-Plough's Polish branch made was unusual (compared to its other donations), and there was a disproportionate increase in the sales of certain cancer drugs in the province where the government director held his post, there was no direct evidence of any actual bribery. Indeed, these were payments that could be called the ultimate in "maintaining a relationship"—the official founded and obviously supported the charity, so the company supported the charity, too. Charitable donations are a well-established way of building community goodwill and corporate branding, but you might as well spend those dollars where they will have the most benefit, right?

Wrong, according to the SEC. The SEC extracted a $500,000 fine from Schering-Plough because "while the payments in fact were made to a bona fide charity, they were made to influence the [d]irector with respect to the purchase of Schering-Plough's products" and, as a result, the payments were improperly recorded in the company's books and records as "donations."

Let's make sure we really understand that: Payments "made to a bona fide charity" that were recorded in the company's books as "donations" violated the FCPA's record-keeping provisions because at least part of the purpose for the donations was to "influence the director," presumably so he would think highly of Schering-Plough and ultimately direct the purchase of more of its products. This is one of my least favorite FCPA cases because, frankly, I think it is flat wrong, although what I think is of little practical import for your corporate compliance purposes. This is the U.S. government's position, and you need to take it seriously.

But indulge me for a paragraph while I take you through what I think is wrong with *Schering-Plough*. To return for a moment to the actual language of the FCPA, it is important to note that the anti-bribery provisions require that the payment or promise to pay be made to *an individual*, not to an entity. As the DOJ itself once wrote in an official opinion statement about the FCPA, where a payment is "made directly to a government entity—and not to any foreign government official—the provisions of the FCPA do not appear to apply." In *Schering-Plough*, the payment was not made to a governmental entity but rather to a charitable entity, but that seems to me to be a distinction without a difference unless there is evidence that the charity is a sham entity that functions solely or substantially as a front for payments to the individual officials. That was certainly not the case in *Schering-Plough*.

But even though it is likely that no violation of the FCPA's anti-bribery provisions occurred in *Schering-Plough*, the SEC still collected a fine because it felt that the motivation behind the payments was insufficiently captured by recording them as "donations." As a result, the SEC took the position that Schering-Plough violated the FCPA's record-keeping and internal controls provisions. The dangers posed by this kind of after-the-fact second-guessing of the word choice used to make accounting entries is discussed in detail in Chapter 10, but for now you need to note that your corporate charitable gift giving can subject you to liability. You need to conduct due diligence on your charitable giving to ensure there is not too close a connection between the charity and any officials who are relevant to your business.

Support for Family Members of Foreign Officials

Perhaps the broad takeaway from *Schering-Plough* is that the U.S. government will look long and hard at any support or assistance you give to a relevant foreign official, even where that assistance is provided in what would be considered a perfectly legitimate manner were it not for the official's position.

Consider this: The founder of your largest customer calls you up and says that his daughter is going to be home from her summer break from college and is interested in learning about marketing (or any of a hundred other business-related things—or maybe nothing at all, maybe she just wants to be out of the house) and asks if you have an intern program. You will probably say that you do, even if you don't, figuring you will find something for her to do just to keep your customer happy. In many cases, you might even offer to pay her, assuming that the customer was just being polite by suggesting an "internship" when she really meant "summer job." This kind of thing, as you know, happens all of the time in every industry, everywhere in the world.

Now imagine that the customer at issue is a state-owned entity or a foreign official with some relevance to your business. Now something that is normally considered perfunctory corporate back-scratching is a potential FCPA problem. Recall our discussion in Chapter 4 regarding engaging businesses owned by relatives of foreign officials. All of the issues raised there come up again here when we consider employing or otherwise directly supporting relatives of foreign officials. This is not just theoretical. The U.S. government brings cases on these kinds of facts.

For example, in the aforementioned *UTStarcom* matter discussed in Chapters 4 and 6, the SEC and DOJ also focused on the company's hiring of individuals affiliated with foreign government customers. The allegation was that UTStarcom ostensibly engaged the relatives to work in the United States, sponsored them for the necessary work visas (very valuable items), but in fact did not require them to perform any work for the company. That is an extreme example, but you can imagine other scenarios where the relative is actually required to show up at the office but is in fact viewed as deadwood or incompetent and never is required to do anything.

One similar area worth noting, because it comes up with some frequency, is support for the children of foreign officials to study in the United States. Awarding them corporate-sponsored "scholarships" or "research grants" that are merely thinly disguised attempts to help pay for their educations is one common technique. Another is to sponsor visas for the children, especially if they are attempting to apply for school or are between programs, so that they can remain in the United States legally during periods when they are not in school. The overall point should be fairly obvious: Any support of this kind will be viewed as a gift to the foreign official parent and should be analyzed and treated as such.

One final point is to note the scrutiny applied to even legitimate hires who have actual expertise and perform work for the company. Often the spouse of an official will work in the same industry and have genuine, valuable skills and experience. This is common throughout the world and in the United States. (Think of all of the lobbyists married to government officials in Washington, D.C.)

As a manager, you want to hire people with the right expertise and the right experience in the right industry. In foreign countries, especially smaller ones, that group of people can be very small and is often incestuous. When new employees are being considered, you may often hear things like: "She really knows the business, and her uncle [husband, father] works in the Ministry of X, so she has good contacts too." This is what we investigators call "a clue." A clue that you should ask more questions and think long and hard about whether the hire will cause potential problems. If it turns out down the road that the relationship was used to exert favorable influence, there will be a lot of second-guessing of otherwise normal corporate activity (all the dinners, the corporate off-sites at the resorts, and other events attended by the foreign official's relative; questions about whether the employee's salary was just too high for her level of experience and whether that excess was actually intended as a "gift" to the official).

Again, these are not just wild scenarios intended to stir up paranoia. Real cases get brought involving these kinds of facts. The *Siemens* case involved just such an example in Argentina. The *Avery Dennison* matter involved such allegations in China. Other historical cases have come up in Egypt and elsewhere, and I have seen it myself in unreported matters in still other countries. Hiring the relatives of foreign officials is an area you have to watch for and be sensitive to.

CHAPTER 8

Know Your Agents
and Consultants

J ust like knowing your customers, knowing the consultants, agents, and the third parties with whom you deal is a central and difficult aspect of FCPA compliance. Shop talk among FCPA lawyers always turns to stories about agents or consultants, with practitioners trying to one-up each other with more and more outlandish tales of obscure, nonsensical, and sometimes downright bizarre third-party engagements they have come across in their practice. My fundamental rule is this: If it does not make sense as a business arrangement, or if the services provided cannot be clearly and quickly explained, you need to ask a lot of hard questions about why that third party was hired.

The most basic things to keep in mind are that a third party does not insulate you from FCPA liability and that everything we have discussed in prior chapters will get you into just as much trouble if done through a third party or consultant. It is true that you cannot be held responsible for the acts of third parties that they were not authorized to perform on your behalf and that you had no ability or reason to know or suspect they would do on your behalf. But therein lies the rub. You should conduct sufficient diligence and exert sufficient controls over your agents to satisfy yourself (and ultimately the SEC and DOJ) that you did everything you could to ensure you were dealing with a legitimate third party and that you could not have known (and did not explicitly or tacitly authorize) whatever bad acts they might have done.

This is no simple task.

General Risks of Consultants and Third Parties

It is a basic fact of business life that you cannot do everything in-house. Agents, consultants, and third-party service providers are essential, and no business can survive without them. Another basic truth is that the vast majority of third parties you deal with are probably legitimate and would not pay bribes on your behalf. So, are you protecting yourself against a remote and unlikely risk? Hardly. Even if only 1 percent of the third parties you deal with pay bribes, that still makes it a certainty that bribery is being committed. Even a small amount of criminal activity is a huge problem. You have to take meaningful steps to stop it.

As an initial matter, I want to be clear that when I refer to "third parties," "consultants," or "agents," I am not using any rigid legal or technical definition. I have seen managers get tripped up by trying to apply narrow definitions of words used in their compliance policies. Don't do that. If you find yourself massaging words to make a distinction like "our policy talks about consultants, but our wholesale distributor is not a consultant, so our FCPA policy does not apply," stop yourself. The FCPA imposes liability on companies for any acts done by anyone on the company's behalf, whether you call them a consultant, agent, distributor, reseller, sales agent, advisor, broker, lobbyist, Tom, Dick, Harry, or anything else. I will primarily use the term "third party" here to make the point that we are talking about the broadest possible category.

On the most basic level, the problem with third parties is the same problem you have with employees: They go out into the world and act on the company's behalf, and those actions create potential liability for the company. The risk with third parties differs, and is generally higher, in that you know your employees and you generally have some understanding of what it is they do and the tasks you have asked them to perform, but with third parties you often know far less or nothing at all. Indeed, that is why you engage the third party—to do something you cannot easily do yourself (or in some cases, to do things you are restricted from doing yourself, such as acts requiring special licensure, like customs brokerage).

Discussions of third parties and the FCPA often focus on "consultants" because many of the cases refer to consultants and it is a vague, catchall term used to describe advisors who otherwise defy description. After all, what else are you going to call the best friend of the minister of oil who seems to do nothing other than simply be the best friend of the minister of oil? Typically, people who do nothing but get you access to decision makers are called consultants, or perhaps lobbyists, but my point is that you could call them anything you want. It is not the nomenclature that is important but the substance of what the third party is actually doing on your behalf.

The starting point for engaging third parties should focus on two fundamental areas: Who are they, and what are they being hired to do? The "Who are they?" piece requires a systematic due diligence process to learn as much as can be learned about them. The "What are they being hired to do?" piece requires a substantive understanding of the engagement and standard practices of contracting with third parties so that you can protect your company and minimize risks. We take each in turn.

Who Are They? Due Diligence on Third Parties

In a perfect world, you would be able to get a detailed background report on any third parties you deal with quickly, cheaply, and well in advance of actually needing their services. But we don't live in that world. We live in a world largely occupied by people wholly unknown to us in countries with poor or nonexistent records about whom we can learn next to nothing that is not based on speculation, rumor, and conjecture, and whom we often need at the last minute to help with a pressing problem. So the basic rule is: Do what you can, do it systematically, and keep good records.

As I have said many times before, it is poor record keeping and a lack of procedures and controls that get most people in trouble. That is the part you can actually do something about. Whether a third party you have engaged ultimately goes off and does something foolish on your company's behalf is something you have much less control over. Proper diligence can go a long way toward insulating your company from liability.

At the outset of any new third-party engagement, you should undertake a process of examining the individual or entity's relationships, reputation, and qualifications. Failure to do this leaves your business open to charges that it failed to institute adequate internal controls. This process need not be overly complex or time consuming, but once instituted, it needs to be followed in every case or the company will again expose itself to charges relating to its controls and procedures (especially where the third party who turns out to be a problem is one hired without following the company's own diligence process). So what does the diligence process look like?

It looks a lot like the discussion we had in Chapter 4 regarding dealing with state-owned entities and companies owned by relatives of foreign officials. First and foremost, you should ask the third parties questions directly. A diligence questionnaire is an easy document to fill out, it will provide you with useful information, and if the third party balks at filling it out and certifying the answers, then you know right away that you might want to look for a different third party to help you. As part of the questionnaire, ask for basic documents that will demonstrate that the company is legitimately formed and registered and holds whatever licenses may be required for the work to be performed.

The second aspect of the diligence effort should be some form of independent background check. These days many companies all over the world perform these services, and some of them do it quite cheaply. Although in many developing countries there may not be databases of public information available against which the names of the company and its principals can be run, other forms of diligence can still be conducted. Have someone go take pictures of the business address—does it look like a real business? Have someone go in and pose as a customer; do the people there look, sound, and act like they are in the business they purport to be in? Do they seem qualified to do what you are engaging them to do? Do the people who work in the office actually know anything about the products or services you will allegedly receive?

This relatively simple exercise can easily protect your company from getting involved in transactions that look really suspicious in hindsight. I cannot tell you the number of times I have had this kind of diligence done after the fact, in circumstances where suspicions have been raised about a third party, and the business address given turns out to be a vacant lot, a crumbling abandoned building, or a business that bears no resemblance to the one purportedly engaged.

Trust me, you want to have a solid answer to the question "Who are they?" before you pay them a lot of money, especially when what they did involved interfacing with a foreign government on your company's behalf.

In addition, to the extent possible, you want to ascertain the third party's general reputation. This can be done through references provided by the third party but should also be independently checked by whoever is doing your background work. Although reputation is by definition based on word of mouth and rumor, it has an important place in the diligence process. After all, the point of diligence is to try to ascertain whether the party at issue is someone with whom you should conduct business and can rely on to act properly. If there is a chorus of industry voices that are negative or skeptical, how will you be able to justify having used the third party if it turns out to be a problem down the road? Reputation matters.

Finally, document the third party's qualification to do the work. With well-known companies, doing this is simple and perhaps unnecessary. A major international law or accounting firm probably needs no diligence in this area, just as for international industry leaders in your business. But local third parties who are relatively unknown need to be vetted. Have they done this kind of work before? Are their rates reasonable given their level of experience? Do other people in the industry use them? Positive answers to these questions will not automatically insulate you from any issues, but they go a long way toward allowing you to say "Hey, we checked these guys out. Our competitors used them, they had a good reputation, and they were well qualified. What else do you want from me?"

These diligence steps are by no means exhaustive or intended to supplant diligence guidance supplied by your legal department of outside counsel based on the specific facts of your business. I hope, however, that these points will raise your understanding of what should be in a diligence process, especially one used to employ third parties in foreign countries.

In addition, whether you need to apply this process to *all* third parties is a matter you have to think through vendor by vendor. You probably do not need a background check on basic suppliers or service providers (e.g., the company that provides your stationery or fixes your copy machine). But anyone who may deal with foreign officials, no matter how little the interaction, should be subjected to some form of diligence process.

What Are They Doing? Contracting with Third Parties

Needless to say, it is always a good idea to have a written contract with the third parties you engage. It sounds obvious, but situations arise all the time where there is either no contract at all or only some preliminary letter of understanding that lacks any of the detail and form provisions typically required by any company's legal or contracts departments.

The usual explanation for the lack of documentation is that the engagement was urgent, there was no time on the front end to hammer out all of the contractual details, and no one ever got back around to formalizing the agreement. "It just seemed unnecessary," people tell me. "The work was already performed." Urgencies arise, to be sure, but depending on what kind of engagement it is, ensuring that you have the proper contractual elements in place can be more important than ever. If the emergency involves interactions with a foreign government, you will want to ensure you have as much protection in place as possible.

Typically, you will want to have four categories of provisions in your contracts to address FCPA concerns:

1. Representations and warranties regarding who the third party is.
2. Very precise language regarding FCPA compliance, specifically defining some of the key elements of the statute and requiring a certification that the third party understands the provisions and intends to comply with them.

3. A contractual ability to check up on the third party, including a requirement that the third party cooperate in any investigation you might undertake and will make available any information you request that relates to the engagement with your company.

4. A right to immediately terminate the agreement if the third party fails to comply with any of the first three categories.

Negotiating any of these provisions can be tricky business, and you should involve the right legal or contracts people in your company or outside counsel who specializes in the FCPA. But certain circumstances arise that should raise serious red flags for you even if you have not yet involved others in the process. First, any third party that simply refuses to sign an agreement not to violate the FCPA should be a nonstarter. Second, you should be very cautious when dealing with anyone who exhibits confusion or recalcitrance in accepting the defined terms in the agreement. Any party that continuously says things like "We have our own definition of government official in our country" is exhibiting a casual attitude toward the contractual terms that should be explicitly corrected, or you may need to find someone else.

At the end of the day, however, you don't want to be too rigid in your approach to contracting. If you have evidence at the time you enter into the contract that the party you are dealing with does not intend to follow it, the protective provisions in your contract may be of little value; U.S. authorities may view them as mere window dressing on a deal you knew was bad from the outset.

In addition to the compliance representations, defining the fee structure and invoicing is critical. When considering the type of fees, the more defined the better. For arrangements involving high-volume work, like customs brokerage services, a detailed fee schedule that defines the services performed for each fee is often a good way to go. Where consultants are concerned, typically hourly fees are preferred, and fees tied to success are disfavored. Although success fees are standard in many industries, especially finder's fees and success fees tied to contract awards or investment amounts, these can look very suspicious where the consultant will have a high level of contact with governmental decision makers. These fees can become the source for kickbacks (where the consultant agrees to share the success fee with the official who awards the business to you).

Although your contracts will have provisions requiring compliance with the FCPA, if the contract also has a provision stating that the consultant gets nothing but expenses reimbursed under the contract yet gets a 3 percent or 5 percent success fee upon wining the contract, two provisions exist with a high degree of tension between them. If the contract value is $10 million, that 3 to 5 percent success fee leaves a lot of cash to spread around among those deciding who will win the contract. It does not matter that the consultant has no money to make the payments until after the deal is done. Promises in advance are the FCPA violation.

Detailed invoicing is also important. Think of our prior discussion about the level of detail you would want to see for the expense reimbursements your own people submit. You need that from your vendors, too. Single-line invoices "for services rendered" should be avoided. The invoice needs to describe exactly what was done and what the fee was for each part of the service. Any expenses being reimbursed should also be supported by the actual receipts for the expenses, as itemized and detailed as possible.

Another provision you want—and can typically get—is a requirement that third parties recertify their FCPA compliance every year. Have them fill out an updated diligence questionnaire and sign a supplemental statement that says they still understand the policies and still intend to abide by them. This ongoing monitoring ensures that as personnel changes at third parties, there is a requirement that they keep all of their people informed and tell you if anything has changed in their organization that might matter to you (like a foreign official taking an ownership interest in a company).

But the contractual provisions that generate the most push-back typically are not the ones requiring compliance with the FCPA. Many third parties are willing to sign those, although I always wonder whether anyone who intends at the outset to pay bribes to get their job done would really have any qualms about misrepresenting their intention to do so by signing a contract that says they won't pay bribes. The real push-back tends to come regarding provisions dealing with cooperation with any investigation and termination rights.

Third parties raise legitimate concerns about these issues. For instance, when requesting the right to inspect the books and records of the third party, many third parties argue that the provisions are too broad, too invasive, or simply too cumbersome. For example, who gets to determine the scope of the review? Even if you limit your right to only those records that relate to the third party's business with you, how, as a practical matter, can third parties separate out those books and records from their general records? Who pays for the cost of the inspection? Can you make copies of the records? Bring in your own third-party experts, such as accountants or lawyers, to view them? And if you decide there is a problem, do you get to terminate the contract at will, without any independent determination?

These are real issues without easy resolutions. As with any contract, all things are negotiable. But the extent to which you abandon or soften your requests should be based on the level of risk associated with the engagement. The company providing your office supplies probably poses little or no actual risk, but you will have much less flexibility with the local lobbyist who is using high-level contacts to help land you a contract directly with a foreign government.

Typically High-Risk Engagements

Generally, the more contact with foreign officials, and the more money at stake, the higher the risk associated with the third-party engagement. But a few categories of engagements tend to come up repeatedly in FCPA cases.

Anytime you engage someone simply for good contacts in a third-world country, you are in a high-risk transaction. The problem is made worse if you try to mask the purpose of the engagement by cloaking it in a consulting contract that purports to be for business or regulatory advice for which the third party has no actual qualification. There is no question that connections matter, especially in corrupt countries were few officials do anything out of the kindness of their hearts or some sense of duty to their country. You might actually need someone purely for contacts so that you can get a meeting with the right people. But be sure to call it what it is and structure the fee agreement accordingly. Giving a percentage of the contract value to someone with no relevant experience who does nothing but make an introduction is hard to justify even under the best of circumstances.

The same goes for engaging relatives of government officials as consultants. This is really the same problem we discussed in Chapter 4 in the context of an accounting firm owned by the daughter of the head of the tax bureau. Having an iron-clad diligence file is important in these situations, even where it is obvious that legitimate services are being provided.

But I have seen situations where the brother-in-law of a high-ranking official is engaged as a consultant. The brother-in-law had no relevant experience in the industry; his sole ability was to get his client into the same room with the official. In these situations, paying the brother-in-law 3 percent of a $20 million contract is almost impossible to justify. I have had managers tell me in similar situations that they thought the fee was completely justified because they "got good value" for the payment—meaning they got the $20 million contract, and still made money even after paying the fee to the consultant.

This may be the investment banker's perspective, and as a purely economic decision, any bribe can be justified as a legitimate cost if you still make money at the end of the day. But this is an extremely dangerous mentality to adopt when doing business with foreign governments and state-owned entities. The decision may be economically rational, but that does not make it legal.

I have seen emails where several managers are discussing the possible employment of a local agent to help them secure a badly needed permit for which they knew the company could not qualify. After going back and forth about the terms of the engagement (including a very large fee request), one of the managers eventually asks what assurances they have that the agent can actually deliver. This is generally not a substantive question about the agent's qualifications—that is, what skills does this agent have such that we should put our faith in his ability—but rather a purely economic question of whether the company is getting good value—meaning results—for the fee it is paying. If you hear or read these conversations, inject some substance into them. Set aside the question of return on the investment in the consultant and ask who the consultant is, what her qualifications are, and why there is any reason to believe she actually can do the work she was hired to do. As a manager, it is ultimately your responsibility to know who you are doing business with and why. If the answer is merely that someone recommended the consultant, but you have no idea what she does to earn his fee, you have controls issues that need to be addressed.

Finally, any agent recommended by the government itself should cause you to ask hard questions. Is the "recommendation" really a "requirement"? And if so, what is so special about this particular agent? When you ask a question like this, you may be met with a response from your people along the lines of; "Well, they say it doesn't *have* to be them, but if we don't use them things will be difficult." Be careful not to turn a blind eye to these kinds of comments. If, at the end of the day, what you are being told by a foreign official is that using someone else might jeopardize your ability to win or retain the business, that is a requirement, not a recommendation. Pretending it is not exposes you to a charge of willful blindness about your understanding of the arrangement.

You should ask questions like:

- Who is the agent related to or affiliated with?
- What service does the agent provide that we cannot provide ourselves?
- Was the need for such an agent always contemplated as part of the deal?

This last question is especially important. If the "requirement" for the consultant seems to come out of the blue and was not part of your original bid or the tender request, you should be particularly suspicious. The unanticipated need for a last-minute consulting contract is a classic pattern that as often as not is revealed to be a sham transaction.

The Sham Consultant

The sham consultant is a perennial problem in the FCPA literature. While most managers can recognize that paying a consulting firm to do absolutely nothing other than collect cash in its bank account and pass it on to influential government officials is a problem, few believe that it can happen in their organization. But think about how many third parties your company engages. Then ask yourself if you can say with certainty what each of those third parties is doing on your behalf—not in generic terms ("They're providing advice") but in specific terms—what meetings they attend, whom they meet with, what conference calls they're on. Who in your organization can say with certainty that they have met these people, spoken to them, seen them in action, and know beyond doubt that they exist and provide real services?

Viewed from that perspective, you can begin to see how many third-party engagements *might* be sham transactions if only because you cannot personally attest to the work performed. Of course, as a manager, you cannot be charged with actually knowing and being able to prove up the legitimacy of anything and everything that happens within your organization. This is where policies and procedures come into play. Having a diligence process that occurs before someone is engaged will ensure that the third party's legitimacy is at least documented in your files. Having proper contracting and approval requirements in place to govern the relationship ensures that you have certain representations and warranties, certain rights, certain compliance and termination clauses, as well as procedures to ensure that invoices are proper and that the right amounts are paid to the right accounts, and only when proper support exists for the payments.

This is not to say that with all of these protections you are guaranteed never to have problems, but it does help you with a defense if you suddenly realize that, despite the existence of a satisfactory paper trail, you have been making payments to a sham consultant who is nothing more than an intermediary for illicit payments. Here are some real-world examples of how sham consultants typically work:

Recall the *Baker Hughes* matter discussed in Chapter 4 where the oil consortium KPO was subject to the control of Kazakhstan's national oil company, Kazakhoil. When Baker Hughes was competing for an oil services contract in Kazakhstan in 1999, it did so without any third-party agents or consultants helping it. The overall project (which included three of its own divisions as well as numerous subcontractors) had an anticipated value of approximately $200 million. Baker Hughes submitted its bid in February 2000, then waited for the bid process to end and for KPO to select a winner. Kazakhoil had final approval over the award of the contract.

In mid-September 2000, the Baker Hughes executives in charge of the bid began hearing "unofficially" that the company was to be the recommended winner. Yet only a week before the final selection was to be announced, the head of the project was informed that in order "to get Kazakhoil approval," Baker Hughes had to agree to pay a 3 percent commission to an agent in London. After scrambling to secure the needed internal approvals and after getting the commission reduced to 2 percent (on this contract and 3 percent on all future contracts), Baker Hughes ultimately agreed to pay the commission in late September 2000. It was awarded the contract the following month.

There was never any question that the agent provided no services or advice of any kind. Baker Hughes conducted no due diligence on the agent, and the agreements with the agent did not go through the firm's normal contracting procedures and did not contain the required FCPA compliance language promulgated by the Baker Hughes legal department. But what makes the facts of *Baker Hughes* even worse, from a compliance standpoint, is that it represents the classic bureaucratic breakdown of internal controls that can easily happen within any company.

On the business side, it appears that none of the Baker Hughes managers wanted to pay the commission and recognized it for what it was: a last-minute effort by Kazakhoil officials to hold the firm hostage and squeeze out some personal benefit for themselves. Yet the managers were concerned about the long-term damage to Baker Hughes' business in Kazakhstan if they refused to go along. As recounted in the Deferred Prosecution Agreement with the DOJ, one executive in Houston went so far as to write an email stating that "unless we pay a commission ... we can say goodbye to this and future business."

This is the classic pressure point that gets many managers in trouble. Sure, Baker Hughes was being held hostage. Failure to pay the agent a commission intended to secure the Kazakhoil recommendation that Baker Hughes win the contract would cause not only a loss of this contract but perhaps all future ones in Kazakhstan because the entire oil industry there was controlled by Kazakhoil. Without paying the commission, Baker Hughes' business in that country might be destroyed. The Baker Hughes managers probably assumed their own careers would fail right along with it. But is this extortion? Were the managers under duress? No.

As the email clearly states, "we can say goodbye to this and future business." They could have walked away from the entire country, but they paid the commission instead.

The managers brought the issue to their legal department, but only after they had already agreed to the commission and signed the contracts with the agent. The legal department forwarded the managers the standard Baker Hughes forms, which included the required FCPA language, but those forms were never used, and the legal department never followed up to confirm that the deal was done and done properly. This is the classic controls failure where the business side does not tell legal the complete story, and legal merely forwards form language to the businesspeople but does not engage in or take over the contracting process. The vacuum left behind permitted the deal to go forward for several years.

Ultimately, Baker Hughes paid the bogus agent $4.1 million and generated $220 million in revenue on the project. When the DOJ and SEC announced the *Baker Hughes* resolutions in early 2007, the firm paid $44 million in fines and penalties, which was then the largest FCPA case in history (As we've discussed, FCPA cases have gotten much larger since then.)

But as I've also mentioned, the cases need not be large to come under government scrutiny. On the opposite end of the spectrum is a similar commission paid by Paradigm, an oil industry software company. In facts eerily similar to those of *Baker Hughes*, Paradigm agreed to pay a commission into a Latvian bank account controlled by a British West Indies agent recommended by an official from Kazakhstan's national oil company (which by then was called KazMunaiGas, not Kazakhoil). In this case, the commission was only $22,250, but once again the agent performed no services of any kind and acted merely as a conduit for funds to go from Paradigm to the Kazakh official.

The Vaguely Understood or Unexplained Consultant

Completely sham transactions are unusual. More common are consulting engagements where the consultants do *something* on your behalf, but it is unclear exactly what. When viewed with hindsight, it is often hard to justify their fees in light of the work they appeared to perform or to explain their fantastic and often quick results.

Think way back to the beginning of this book when we discussed the customs agent situation where you flew a replacement part to your Bangalore factory only to find it stuck at the airport in a mire of opaque and glacial customs processes. The customs officer suggested an agent who specialized in a rapid clearance process you knew nothing about. You hired the agent, paid him a high fee, and just an hour or two later your part was yours to take. This was not a sham transaction. The customs agent clearly did something on your behalf, but what? The result was great and quick, the fee was high, and the recommendation came from the very customs officer who was holding up your shipment. All of these are suspicious facts under the circumstances, but the central problem isn't that there are suspicious facts—it's that *in light of those facts*, you have no ability to say what the agent did.

Because you cannot explain, and indeed do not understand, what the agent did, the assumption is that he did something bad. Any good FCPA lawyer will argue that there is no direct evidence that the agent paid a bribe—that whether the agent paid an official to get a good result is simply unknowable and that you or your company cannot be held criminally responsible in light of this unknown. But that may not save you.

As mentioned numerous times before (and as discussed in detail in Chapter 10), the inability to clearly document an answer to the question "What happened?" places you in the crosshairs of the FCPA's internal controls and record-keeping provisions. Even if you can convincingly make the case that you were negligent, inattentive, or genuinely did not understand the transaction you were involved in (all of which reflect poorly on a manager's abilities), your company may still be on the hook because the records simply cannot explain what happened. This becomes a live issue in the real world because real-life regulatory examples are often much more complex than the simple Bangalore customs clearance hypothetical.

Recall our discussion of the global investigation into logistics, freight forwarding, and customs clearance provider Panalpina from Chapter 3. One of the many issues in those cases was the importation of drilling rigs and oil field equipment—often very large and not easily moved pieces of equipment worth tens of millions of dollars—that were subject to a customs regime that may or may not have permitted the "local processing fees," "interventions," or "evacuations" that Panalpina provided.

Naturally, companies outsourced the customs clearance work for their equipment and generally had little or no understanding of what the actual rules for customs importation were. This, of course, is the exact reason companies typically hire outside experts or consultants: They cannot navigate all regulatory processes on their own.

That is the central problem with consultants and the FCPA. Because you often hire them to help your company with things you do not understand yourself, it is difficult to monitor what they do on your company's behalf or to ensure that everything is sufficiently documented and explainable. Let's look at one more example, just to view the problem from another angle.

Say your company lands a large contract for an infrastructure project in a Middle East country. The contract contains an "offset" requirement, essentially mandating that a certain percentage of the contract value be reinvested within the country. This can take the form of hiring local contractors or investing in some completely unrelated business activity, so long as the value of the "local content" is certified by an oversight board that manages the local reinvestment requirements for all such contracts within the country. Because of the technical nature of the project, your company decides it cannot hire sufficient local contractors to satisfy the requirement. Through one of the government officials involved in the bid process, you learn of a consulting firm in London that is known to help companies find suitable local investments that satisfy the local content criteria. For a percentage of the amount invested, the London firm manages the entire process and guarantees that the investments it finds will be approved by the oversight board. Your company does nothing other than deposit the required sum in an escrow account in London and later receives approval for the reinvestment from the oversight board.

Unlike the cases of *Baker Hughes* or *Paradigm*, the consultant in this example appears to provide an actual service.

But what? How do you satisfy yourself that the real arrangement between the London consultant and the oversight board is not simply an agreement to pay most of the reinvestment money to the oversight board members personally, or to invest in businesses they own, in exchange for their approval? This is where due diligence and contracting process are critical. To some extent, it may not matter what they did with the money so long as you can conclusively demonstrate that you looked into them, that they were legitimate and reputable, and that your contract with them contained sufficient controls that they would have had to go to great lengths to fake an investment and deceive you with it.

Distributors and Buy/Sell Arrangements

Many managers share the misconception that their distributors and resellers do not pose FCPA risks. Sometimes that's true, but often it is not. In situations where a distributor purchases your company's goods and sells them to its own customers for whatever margin it can get, without any further contact or involvement from your company, it may well be a low-risk relationship. Indeed, in those situations, you may have no idea who the ultimate end users of your product are.

But often the interactions between a company and its distributors are much more complex. The more involvement you have with your distributors, and the more you know about who their ultimate customers are, the more you expose yourself to liability for their actions. Local distributors are commonly used as conduits for bribes because when a distributor makes the payment, the problematic transaction occurs wholly outside of the manufacturer's books and records. The next transaction is a common scenario.

Your company manufactures technical equipment that is used in a wide variety of industrial and research settings. Each foreign market where your products are sold is served by an exclusive distributor. However, because of the technical aspects of your products, you often make your own people available for educational seminars and training, conducted along with your distributors, to ensure that repeat and potential customers are properly educated about the technical aspects of the products. When a state-controlled university system in a country served by a specific distributor contacts your sales team directly to discuss a large purchase, your sales team negotiates directly with the university. The purchasing agent for the university system then notes that several of your competitors are offering "rebates" in the form of a small percentage of the contract price to be paid directly to the purchasing agent. Your sales team, knowing that you could never make such a payment, takes the already negotiated deal to the distributor in that country and has the distributor make the sale and pay the "rebate" back to the university purchasing agent.

In some ways, this is the perfect transaction. On your company's books, the transaction looks like any other transaction. Your distributor ordered product from you and ultimately sold it. The distributor gets a sale without having to do any legwork and probably still makes a profit even after paying the rebate out of the normal profit it would make on such a sale. No paper trail of any kind exists in your company's accounting records that could ever be construed as an FCPA violation. And yet your salespeople agreed to make a payment directly to the purchasing agent for a state-controlled university in exchange for a large purchase of equipment. They then routed it through your distributor to make it look like a normal sale. This happens more than you might think.

The bottom line is to be mindful of how much interaction you have with your distributors, sales agents, and the like. The more you participate in joint marketing, education, training, and promotional activities with your distributors, the higher the risk and the more control and oversight you need to exert over them.

Dual Roles: Government Officials Moonlighting as Consultants

Another common problem is that officials sometimes blur the distinction between "public" and "private" by holding themselves out as consultants to help you comply with the very regulatory process they oversee. They may refer to a side business of some kind that the official either owns or has some murky affiliation with, or sometimes a government official will suggest the use of a particular vendor who is "preferred" or "very experienced" in the relevant area. Often it is not clear what services the vendor will provide or what relationship the vendor has with the official who is making the suggestion. If questions are asked about why that particular consultant, you may well be told that you can use who you want, but that these recommended people are the best. The implication is that only the suggested consultant can ensure a smooth process or guaranteed results.

You may want to stay away from these arrangements whenever you can. As we discussed in Chapter 4 when dealing with businesses owned by foreign officials or their relatives, the safest course is often to look for another vendor that does not have that relationship. This is not always possible, but it generally will be. As a practical matter, any such engagement presents the same issues as any consulting engagement. You need to document the consultant's legitimacy and put controls in place to ensure FCPA compliance. But whenever you are dealing with a consultant who is affiliated with a foreign official in some way, you start the process with a distinct and sometimes insurmountable disadvantage.

Finally, one related area to look out for is hidden or unexplained fees in connection with government contracts. These may not relate to consultants or third parties but rather to "ancillary" services of some kind purportedly provided by the agency itself. Often this comes up when the agency purports to offer "consulting services" or advice relating to its own regulations. So long as the funds really are being paid to an official government bank account, it is harder to show an FCPA violation, but you need to be careful. Here's an example:

A foreign official in charge of awarding a contract for a major new public works project conducts a public bid process. During the bid period, she calls you into her office for a bid meeting (or sends one of her minions around to your office) and informs you that all bidders are required to add a processing fee of 5 percent onto their final bids. She explains that because the amount is fixed, it will not affect the bid process, as all bids will be increased by the same percentage. She further informs you that the processing fee is to be remitted to a "special fund" within her department and proceeds to provide a vague description of how the funds are to be remitted, which boils down to a process or an account that does not clearly go into the government treasury.

This situation is more common than you might imagine. Often such arrangements stem from very legitimate governmental issues. Certain agencies might be "self-funded," for example, and need to raise operational revenue by whatever means they can. Others may have severely underpaid officials who use the money to supplement their meager incomes and not necessarily to bestow favor on any particular company or individual. But even where the roots of such an arrangement are not wholly nefarious, you have to be very skeptical. Most officials will be unwilling to put these arrangements in writing, clearly spelling out the purpose for the funds and where they are to be paid. Needless to say, you should assume the worst in such cases until clearly proven otherwise.

CHAPTER 9

So What *Can* You Do?

Facilitating Payments and Other Exceptions

I often hear managers say things like: "It was a facilitating payment, so it was fine." Maybe. But knowing the difference between a true facilitating payment and a bribe is the key, and many managers simply do not know the difference. As discussed in Chapter 1, facilitating, or "grease," payments are for truly nondiscretionary government functions, and very few actions are totally nondiscretionary.

There are three categories of exceptions or affirmative defenses to the FCPA, and all of them have already been mentioned in prior chapters:

1. The facilitating payments exception
2. The affirmative defense for promotional expenses
3. The affirmative defense allowing actions that are lawful under the written laws of the official's home country

I touch on each of these briefly here to round out the prior discussions and to make sure that the contours and limitations of each are understood.

With all the emphasis on how tricky and unreliable these exceptions and defenses are, I'll start with some good news:

There are payments to government officials that clearly are legal. Indeed, the FCPA mentions some of them by name.

Things You Clearly Can Pay For

As previously discussed, the facilitating payments exception applies to "routine governmental action," which is defined in the statute to include a laundry list of typically nondiscretionary functions. I find it helpful to break the enumerated nondiscretionary services into two categories: those that relate to essential health, safety, and governmental services and those that do not. The four essential health, safety, and governmental services listed in the statute as "routine governmental action" are:

1. Providing police protection
2. Providing mail pickup and delivery
3. Providing phone service, power, and water supply
4. Loading and unloading cargo

The statute also includes a catchall provision for "actions of a similar nature," which can be relied on for services that go directly to the health and safety of your employees. If you need to pay the fire department (or make a donation to the firemen's fund) to ensure it will respond in an emergency, that is unlikely to get the Department of Justice riled up. The same would go for ambulance services, security provided by the government-controlled export zone police, or payments to get the trash hauled away from the sidewalk in front of your business.

If it is a service that is provided by the government in the country where you operate and it relates directly to your ability to keep your people and your business safe and functioning at a basic level, the facilitating payments exception may apply so long as there are no other facts that indicate that you are really paying for something else. (If you pay the police chief because he is the brother of the tax inspector whom you are trying to get to overlook certain violations, that is not going to pass muster.)

But the FCPA defines "routine governmental action" to include other categories that are harder to pin down. They do not fit into the essential health, safety, or governmental functions category because, although they are provided by the government, they are not necessarily essential to protecting your employees or your business. They are primarily administrative and require a more complex analysis of nondiscretionary action than simply determining whether or respond to an emergency call, or whether to deliver someone's mail or turn their power or water on.

These "routine governmental actions" often have requirements that you or your business or employees have to fulfill before the government official is "obligated" to do anything, and often the determination of whether those requirements have been satisfied is left to the discretion of the official. And this determination is the central aspect of these "routine governmental functions" that must be analyzed by someone inside or outside of your company who is familiar with the FCPA before any of these payments can be correctly categorized as facilitating payments.

As set out in the statute, routine governmental actions that *may* allow facilitating payments are:

1. Obtaining permits, licenses, or other official documents to qualify a person to do business in a foreign country
2. Processing governmental papers, such as visas and work orders
3. Protecting perishable products or commodities from deterioration
4. Scheduling inspections relating to contract performance or transport of goods
5. Actions of a similar nature

Although the phrase "actions of a similar nature" is open-ended, the government takes the position (and most practitioners agree) that the essential component of any routine governmental action is that it is nondiscretionary in nature. If the foreign official must make a judgment call of some kind in connection with the official action, then any payment made to ensure that she exercises that judgment in a certain way will not qualify as a facilitating payment.

The central difference between the group of five actions and the group of four actions mentioned before them is that the four actions generally require no discretionary decisions by the official whereas the five actions often do. For this reason, it is on the group of five that we focus our attention.

What a Facilitating Payment Is and Is Not

With the five potentially discretionary actions in mind, you can see that many "routine governmental actions" set out in the FCPA actually do very little to guide behavior as to specific potential facilitating payments. In most cases, you will need very precise factual information about the situation on the ground before a legal determination about the FCPA can be made.

Many of the five actions just mentioned have been discussed throughout this book as examples of administrative processes that can and often do lead to FCPA problems. Let's walk back through them quickly to ensure we understand their typical discretionary aspects.

Obtaining Permits, Licenses, or Other Official Documents to Qualify a Person to Do Business in a Foreign Country

I discussed this in Chapter 3. There we went through the significance that operating licenses may have because they often contain restrictions or descriptions that have long-term consequences on your ability to run your business: what kind of business, the amount of local sales, the amount of exports, the allocation of warehouse and office space, the number of expat employees. Whether, and to what extent, to grant modifications of these provisions is inherently discretionary.

Similar issues exist with respect to all other forms of licenses and permits. In many developing countries, the processes for applying for and obtaining permits are opaque and the application requirements are unclear. This leaves the processes open to abuses and shakedowns. To make matters worse, you may learn that you engaged a consultant to help you with your licensing, thereby adding another layer of risk to an already risky area. If you use a third party to walk you through a regulatory scheme because you do not understand the scheme, how can you ever be certain you know where your money is going? This is where diligence on your third-party agents becomes critical, especially if their fees are far in excess of the costs for the actual licenses or permits.

Processing Governmental Papers, Such as Visas and Work Orders

First of all, "governmental papers" is such a broad category that it offers no guidance at all. Filling out an inspection form could technically be "processing" a "government paper," and payments to get good results on an inspection are clearly an FCPA violation. If you are merely making a small payment to get an inspection or work order scheduled, that is permissible, but think about whether you will be able to clearly show that all you paid for is the appointment. When viewed with hindsight, it is often difficult to decouple the payment to schedule the inspection from the positive results of the inspection itself. Everyone will say, "Of course you passed the inspection, you paid the guy!"

Beyond that, we already know from the *DynCorp* case discussed in Chapter 3 that visa processing can lead to FCPA problems. Recall that DynCorp subcontractors may have paid, in total, about $300,000 around the world to obtain visas and licenses. What they paid in any individual country was presumably far less. If you operate in a developing country, you might find that you easily spend $10,000 or $20,000 per year on expatriate visas, even if you have relatively few expat employees in the country. You may well do this through an agent, which makes assessing the nondiscretionary aspects of the visa process that much more difficult.

Protecting Perishable Products or Commodities from Deterioration

This is a favorite example of practitioners, often used as a model of the petty bureaucratic shakedowns that occur all over the world. Your shipment of bananas is sitting on the docks at the port. All of the paperwork is done. Your truck is idling in the parking lot, waiting to haul them to your customers. But the customs official simply will not sign the paperwork releasing them from the customs storage area. The customs agent knows they will rot and become worthless very quickly. Time is on his side. The longer he waits, the more likely you are to pay him to sign the paperwork. This is the situation this language was intended to cover.

But think again about documentation. Will your files make it clear that all you were paying for was to get the official to sign paperwork he was already technically obligated to sign? This is common in the customs clearance process, which often involves a third-party agent who handles clearance on your behalf. Once again, you need to be certain that the invoices clearly reflect payments of this nature and that you have a clear understanding of what those payments are for.

Scheduling Inspections Relating to Contract Performance or Transport of Goods

We have discussed inspections in numerous places. The difficulty of teasing out a distinction between scheduling the inspection and ensuring that you pass the inspection makes this a very dangerous area. To be sure, there will be times a payment needs to be made just to ensure you can get onto an official's schedule. This is what the statute contemplates.

But before you just assume that the appointment is all you are getting, think about how you will explain the transaction years later. As a manager, you probably have no real involvement with the inspection itself, so you will not be able to speak to what was actually done (or even whether an actual inspection was conducted or whether the inspector just approved it in exchange for the payment).

In prior chapters, I posed rhetorical questions all managers should ask themselves when they take over a new business unit; one was whether the regulatory compliance history you are inheriting seems too good to be true. After all, every business has regulatory problems from failed inspections, to expired permits, to late or missing paperwork. If you never have these kinds of problems, it may not be because your business is a perfectly run operation, especially if you are in a developing country. If your business unit has a history or pattern of paying to schedule inspections and then always seems to pass them with flying colors, do some investigating of your own. You may learn that the facilitating payments exception is being used as cover for what are not facilitating payments at all.

Promotional Expenses

This defense was discussed at length in Chapter 6. Recall that there the point was that the expenditure must be "reasonable and bona fide" and that it had to relate to "the promotion, demonstration, or explanation of products or services" or to "the execution or performance of a contract." We walked through a number of examples having to do with travel and entertainment expenses. We won't go over those again here, but we will discuss a few other common scenarios that come up all the time.

One of them has to do with corporate gifts. These arise in several routine contexts. The first is high-level corporate and government interactions that are generally connected to a larger business purpose. For example, if you have just opened a large manufacturing facility in an industrial zone outside Jakarta, your CEO and other senior officers might come to pay a visit, meet the employees, and engage in the kind of normal corporate goodwill activities that occur on these trips, such as meeting local officials connected to the industrial zone or the city as a whole.

It is common to give token gifts to the attendees at such meetings. Most practitioners agree that these gifts are permissible so long as they are "reasonable and bona fide" and they contain some element that promotes the company (such as a company logo). As I have cautioned before, that does not give you carte blanche to put the company logo on a Rolex—that would be neither reasonable nor bona fide—but anything you normally give out to company employees is likely permissible (T-shirts, gym bags, small and inexpensive personal items).

Many practitioners also like to get some assurance that the company has no business pending with the particular officials at the time the gift is given. My own view is that this is nice but does not offer much FCPA protection. Remember that as an affirmative defense and not an exception, you essentially admit to the statutorily prohibited activity in order to invoke the defense. It is often difficult, if not impossible, to articulate in a meaningful way or with any real assurance that good relationships with high-level officials have no real benefit to your business. For example, the official who oversees the entire industrial zone where your factory is may not be someone with whom you conduct particular pieces of regulatory business, but you are constantly under that official's jurisdiction and, in that sense, the official is *always* in a position to help you in some way. At the very least, maintaining a good relationship with such an official is beneficial.

A similar situation comes up at contract signings. Can you give a similar gift to the official or officials present at a formal contract award or signing—something to commemorate the occasion? Because such a situation obviously involves the direct award of government business to the company, there is a natural tendency to be more suspicious of any gift given in that context. But this is also a situation where it seems appropriate to promote your company and its commitment to the project. As long as the gifts are the kind of low-value promotional items just mentioned, I generally do not get too exercised about them, and I have never seen any government enforcement people get upset either.

But the bottom line for these or any other scenarios is that the gift really must be reasonable—meaning low value. Listen to your gut. If it makes you uncomfortable, raise the issue to a broader audience within your company. Some companies have a range of corporate gifts available through certain vendors, some of which can be quite nice (Tiffany vases, Steuben glass pieces, Waterford crystal bowls, etc.). These gifts may well be inappropriate, especially if they are reserved for significant achievements within the company (employee of the year, salesperson of the year, twentieth anniversary with the company, etc.). If your company views a gift as "high value"—meaning it's reserved for significant achievements—then it probably does not qualify as an appropriate gift for these purposes.

Affirmative Defense for Actions That Are Legal under the Written Laws of the Local Country

As a practical matter, this is an affirmative defense of almost no value. I have never heard of anyone relying on it, and I am unaware of the U.S. government ever giving anyone a pass based on this defense. But it does exist.

Specifically, the FCPA states that it is an affirmative defense to the statute if

> *the payment, gift, offer, or promise of anything of value that was made, was lawful under the written laws and regulations of the foreign official's, political party's, party official's, or candidate's country.*[1]

Read it closely. Many people have found this just as puzzling as you probably do.

As I have mentioned before, even the most corrupt nations generally have written statutes prohibiting bribery, and even an absence of written prohibitions is not the same as written laws expressly *permitting* bribery—which is what the FCPA requires. The central distinction is that an *absence* of written laws prohibiting bribery is not the same as a written law expressly *permitting* bribery. Because this defense is never applied, there is little in the way of guidance on it.

But certain scenarios come close to invoking it. For example, South Korea's Supreme Court has expressly held that there is a *de minimus* exception to that country's written prohibition on giving gifts to public officials. This is intended to permit routine, low-value gifts given at traditional holidays and at traditional gift-giving events (weddings, birth of children, etc.). In the United

---

[1] See Appendix 1, Sec. 78dd-1(c)(1).

States, decisions of the U.S. Supreme Court are considered "law" although they are obviously not statutes. Does a written opinion of the South Korean Supreme Court count as the "written laws" of the country for purposes of invoking this obscure FCPA defense? It is certainly not a crazy position to take, if you had to take it.

But the point here is that you would not want to make that judgment on your own. Forget that this defense exists. Do not be the test case. Have your legal department make the hard calls like these.

Shakedowns and Threats

Although not in the statute, another category that comes up from time to time can be referred to generally as shakedowns, threats, or abuses of power. What I am talking about here are genuine abuses that cannot reasonably be said to be within the official duties of the government employee.

Let me start by distinguishing this from another category of behavior we have already discussed: nondiscretionary decisions. Recall the example of the stubborn customs agent who simply refuses to stamp your passport when you have all of the required visas and stamps issued from that government's consulate. The official wants $20 to do what he is already obligated to do. Certainly that's a shakedown, but you are not paying him to exercise any discretion in your favor, you are just paying him to do his job, which arguably is not even a payment subject to the FCPA (and is certainly a facilitating payment).

Here we are talking about behavior that is outside the bounds of the official's duties. Perhaps I can illustrate with a story.

I was in Jakarta in 2001—not long after September 11—and some colleagues and I went to eat at a restaurant in the old

Dutch part of the city. Perhaps foolishly, we took no security precautions and only had one person with us who spoke Bahasa. The restaurant was in a large restored colonial building and we took a long time eating, ordering extra dishes just to try them, drinking a lot of cocktails, and generally being obnoxious Americans.

As our taxis waited for several hours outside the restaurant, apparently word got around that there were a bunch of rich Americans in the restaurant, drinking and spending with reckless abandon. When we finally left, late in the evening, the cars pulled out onto a wide but oddly empty boulevard—Jakarta has some 15 or 20 million people in the metropolitan area, and its streets are rarely empty. It was one of those moments when you realize that something is definitely wrong, though you can't quite figure out what it is in time to do anything about it. Not that we could have spoken to the taxi driver anyway to tell him to go another way.

Moments later, the street was swarmed with at least a hundred soldiers or policemen—we were never really sure which they were—each brandishing fully automatic Pindad assault rifles and batons. There were so many that our cars had to slow to avoid running over them, and they began thumping on the cars with their batons, which apparently means something like "Stop! Or we'll shoot."

Once they had us out of the cars, the shakedown began. The senior officer, gray-haired, with a rumpled uniform and a well-practiced scowl, began yelling for our passports. Duly produced, he flipped through a few of them and began shaking his head. His men lined us up by the cars. Our interpreter began trying to negotiate, but all the old man would say was that we had big problems, our papers were not right, and we would have to go with them to sort it all out.

Although none of us had ever been to an Indonesian jail, we were not eager for the new experience. We also knew the entire pretext was bogus. We were legally in the country and, whatever kind of officials these were, they were not customs or immigration officers. But what difference does any of that make when you're outnumbered a dozen to one by machine gun–toting thugs on a dark street in Jakarta? And it isn't like a bunch of pasty, out-of-shape lawyers are going to put up a fight in any event. How sad would that be?

So it came down to money.

Fortunately, our interpreter proved an adept negotiator. We would have been happy to hand over what we had, but she promptly told us that would be outrageous (as if everything up to that point had been acceptable). At the end of the day, we handed over 500,000 rupiah to be allowed to get back into our taxis and drive away. Although we never learned who ratted us out, we did learn a valuable lesson: At 500,000 rupiah for the nine of us, the price of freedom, at least back then, came out to about five bucks a head.

But did we violate the FCPA? No.

The focus of the FCPA is the payment or promise of something in exchange for official influence to either obtain or retain business or to secure an improper advantage over your competitors. What happened to us on the roadside in Jakarta was none of those things. Surely the government of Indonesia does not condone the baseless detention and harassment of foreign businesspeople. Indeed, what that senior officer was doing in having his men hold us at gunpoint until we coughed up enough cash to satisfy him was surely illegal under Indonesian law. But as we've seen, that alone does not mean there is no FCPA violation. (After all, nearly every receipt of a bribe is illegal under the laws of the country where it is received.)

Just because they were government officials—they were either police or military personnel—does not mean they were acting in an official capacity. The key distinction is that when you pay a tax official to overlook a tax violation, or you pay a kickback to the government purchasing agent whose job is to make decisions about what products to buy, you are paying an official to make a decision that relates to his or her official duties. When you pay a military official who has no right to detain you simply to stop detaining you, you are dealing with a thug who is using his power over you (a power conferred by the machine gun, not a government title) to abuse and intimidate you.

There is also a separate distinction to be made in that the payment was not business related. Although we were there on a business trip, our payment really had nothing to do with obtaining or retaining business or securing an unfair competitive advantage. The payment was to secure our personal freedom. You may recall that way back in Chapter 1 we discussed "Defenses that don't work," the last of which was the concept of extortion. One of the main reasons extortion is typically not an available defense is because the threats made are usually against the business, not the individual employees. In this situation, extortion came into play because the threat was against the individuals and not the business. The military officer had no idea who we were or what our business was, nor did he care. It was irrelevant to him. All he knew was that we were foreigners and we appeared to have money to spare. He threatened and intimidated us, at gunpoint, until we handed over enough money to make him go away (which turned out to be a paltry sum to us). This is surely extortion, and one could argue it comes close to crossing the line into garden-variety robbery.

The bottom line then is that threats like these that are personal in nature are categorically different from the kind of corrupt behavior we have discussed throughout this book. But be mindful of the narrow set of circumstances to which this example applies.

First, you need to be behaving legally in every way. If you do not have the proper visa to be in the country, the official probably has a right to detain you. You are essentially an illegal immigrant in the country. You need to be under a sufficient level of threat. Guns and other weapons being bandied about is a good fact here. Mere inconvenience (*You try standing in that line! There's no air conditioning in there!*) is not going to cut it. I generally tell people that the threat needs to be real and immediate enough so that even government prosecutors are likely to agree that they would have made the same payoff you did had they been in the same situation.

CHAPTER 10

Keeping Good Records and Maintaining Good Procedures

As a technical matter, the record-keeping and internal controls provisions have a different jurisdictional hook than
the anti-bribery provisions. For just about any reader of this
book, this is a distinction without a difference, but it is worth
at least noting here. The FCPA requires "every issuer which has
a class of securities registered" on a U.S. stock exchange and
"every issuer which is required to file reports pursuant to section
78o(d)" of the Securities and Exchange Act to comply with the
FCPA's record-keeping and internal controls provisions. These
provisions do not apply to individuals, only to certain kinds of
companies. As an individual U.S. citizen, I do not need to keep
good records of my personal activities (indeed, I don't need to
keep any records at all), but I still cannot commit acts of bribery
when I travel abroad.

But most managers, sales, marketing, or finance people
reading this book do not need to concern themselves with this
distinction. If you work for a company that is publicly traded
in the United States, the record-keeping and internal controls
provisions apply. And, in any event, if your employer has asked
you to read this, it has already decided you need to know it
anyway.

As we saw back at the beginning with the *Siemens* settlement, the record-keeping and controls provisions provide the hook for corporate FCPA violations. The burden of proof is lower, and regulators need not prove any actual bribery occurred. But *Siemens* is not the best example of how broad the books and records provisions are. Most people would agree that routing funds through a labyrinth of bank accounts to create a slush fund for illicit payments results in inaccurate books and records. In that regard, *Siemens* is an easy case from a books and records perspective. The much more troubling example is the case of *Schering-Plough*.

Recall from Chapter 7 that the *Schering-Plough* matter involved a Polish subsidiary of the well-known pharmaceutical company that made donations to a charity that restored castles and historical sites in Poland. The charity was founded and supported by an official who had influence over the purchase of pharmaceuticals in a certain region of Poland. The donations were larger than the subsidiary's typical donations, but there was no dispute that the charity was legitimate and did legitimate charitable work. During the time at issue, the subsidiary saw an uptick in the sales of certain cancer drugs in the region the official oversaw.

Although the donations were recorded in the books as donations, the SEC extracted a fine and settlement from Schering-Plough because, it contended, at least part of the purpose for the donations was to influence the official. Thus, they were not purely donations in the strictest sense of the word. The central issue in *Schering-Plough* then was whether the language used to record the expense was accurate enough. There was no dispute that it was accurate in a high-level sense. After all, the company made donations to a bona fide charity and recorded the expenses as a "donations" in its books. Essentially, the SEC appeared to be saying "That's all true, but ..."

But what? But part of the motivation was to build a good relationship with a key official? But the donations just smelled bad? I am not trying to be facetious. I focus on *Schering-Plough* to get you to think about its broad implications and what it means for a busy manager charged with running a business.

Most people recognize, and indeed readily agree, that wholly fictitious records are a problem. Recall our prior discussion of the use of travel agencies in China to conceal illicit or improper expenses. If the actual bill is $25,000, but they fold in an extra $5,000, spread it across all the expense categories (food, banquet rooms, audio-visual equipment), and hand your sales manager $4,500 (after keeping $500 for their troubles), almost everyone immediately sees how the resulting $30,000 invoice used to support the expense for a "seminar" or "training" in the books results in a violation of the FCPA's books and records provisions. The invoice simply is not an accurate representation of what really occurred.

But the *Schering-Plough* case casts a much broader net. There the SEC basically questioned the motivation behind an otherwise legitimate and correctly recorded expense. Essentially, the argument was that it was *more* than just a donation. It was somehow a gift to the official because the official was involved with the charity and somehow derived a personal benefit from the donations. Perhaps the official was altruistically happy (the horror!) at the prospect of his favorite charity being able to do more. This strikes me as a dubious theory, but it is one that you, as a manager, have to take seriously. Indeed, record-keeping and internal controls violations make an appearance in virtually every FCPA case. They are ubiquitous, and the notion that the U.S. government will probe for some deeper meaning beyond the words on the face of the documents themselves is troubling and far-reaching.

Also of note is the previously mentioned *Schnitzer Steel* matter. There the SEC brought an enforcement action for kickbacks paid to the managers of wholly *private* steel mills. The basis for those charges was that "Schnitzer violated the FCPA by failing to properly account for and disclose the bribes in its internal records and public filings." Kickbacks to private companies or individuals may violate commercial bribery laws, but they do not violate the FCPA's criminal anti-bribery provisions. I mention this only to underscore a point I made earlier: The FCPA's record-keeping and controls provisions apply to *all* corporate activities, not just those involving FCPA-related activity.

The Metaphysics of Record Keeping

What then is the true nature of an expense? How can you avoid the after-the-fact second-guessing that *Schering-Plough* embodies? This is no small task. Most employees outside of the accounting or finance departments never give much thought to how expenses are recorded, other than to ask whose budget the expense comes out of.

But *Schering-Plough* requires companies to ask questions that get behind the basic expense documentation to ensure that the records capture the true essence of the expense. What makes this such a difficult task is the sheer volume of expenditures any sizable company has. That, combined with the extremely mundane nature of most of them and the fact that they are generally processed by low-level employees in the accounting department, means that companies are left searching for needles in the proverbial haystack, using employees who may be extremely uninterested in actually finding them.

The simple truth is that you cannot engage in an inquisition over every expense. The best you can do is build a corporate culture that understands and cares about these issues, and then educate your accounting people to focus on the highest-risk areas and encourage them to be thoughtful about expenses incurred in those categories. Once they understand where the risks are, some level of substantive review should be undertaken beyond merely checking the boxes to see if it was approved with the correct internal form or whether all the required parties have signed the approval. The fundamental question should always be: Do these documents make sense, and do they adequately explain the nature of the transaction?

All of the examples discussed in this book are fertile ground for books and records issues. Setting aside the issue of wholly fabricated documentation for a moment, let's focus on expenses that most typically raise the kinds of issues seen in *Schering-Plough*. Most of these are discussed in detail in chapters of their own, but here we focus solely on the issue of the documents that result from these transactions.

Gifts, Travel, Meals, and Entertainment

Gifts, travel, meals, and entertainment expenses are inherently risky because, unlike *Schering-Plough*, the expense typically results from something given directly to the official, not an intermediary organization, such as a charity or other institution. As a result, it is much easier to raise questions about the motivation or purpose underlying the expense. There is no need to draw the kind of suspect conclusions about the relationship between the official and the intermediary that were required in *Schering-Plough*. In these circumstances, there is no question that the official received a benefit, so the only question the SEC or DOJ needs to ask is: Why?

- Why did you take this official to dinner? (Once? Three times? Twenty times?)
- Why did you give that official a gift basket?

- Why did these officials fly to this resort and stay there for three days, all at company expense?
- Why did the company pay for a night on the town?

The documents themselves rarely answer these questions. Typically they consist of only an expense reimbursement form and a supporting receipt from a restaurant, hotel, or bar. The expense form may require only a list of attendees without any description that could help answer the questions just set out.

The central books and records problem then is trying to ensure that the company knows the answers and can document them in a way that will be meaningful after the fact when questions are raised. One key way to do this is to require advance approval by someone in your company who understands the FCPA. The approval process creates a record of its own and should contain a written description of the purpose for the meal/gift/travel, etc. The advance approval process also acts as an internal control mechanism to ensure that blatantly problematic transactions are stopped before they proceed beyond the planning stage (before any offer is made, one hopes).

Completeness and specificity of the records are also important. Ensure that all related documentation is retained. For meals, this may simply be the receipt from the restaurant, but for travel, it may include a broader range of documents such as plane tickets, hotel receipts, and agendas for the meetings attended. As for the level of detail, the more the better. Anytime the records fail to fully explain a transaction, you have potential problems. You want the records to paint a clear and unassailable picture of what happened and why. Every element of vagueness increases the chances of a record-keeping problem by increasing the level of suspicion surrounding the transaction.

For example, a single-page invoice from a travel agent for plane tickets and a hotel room indicating that the passenger was a particular official will only raise questions. It is too thin of a

record to make clear that the expense was for a legitimate purpose. The record does nothing to address fundamental questions
like:

- Was this a vacation or a business meeting?
- Why was the company footing the bill, even if it was a
  business meeting?
- If it was a business meeting and there was a legitimate reason for the company to pay for the costs, what corroborating
  documentation exists?

It is this last question that is most important. As I have said
before, these cases often come up well after the underlying
events occurred, when few, if any, of the original participants
are left at the company. Those few who remain may have little
or no recollection of the facts (and may have a strong incentive
to lie or suddenly be unable to remember what happened). In
these situations, which arise frequently, all that remains is the
cold documentary record to explain where the money went. If
that record leaves basic questions unanswered or is subject to
more than one interpretation, you have a potential books and
records problem.

Instead of a one-page invoice from the travel agent, ideally what you would want would be the advance request and
approval that explained why the expenses were necessary; a
detailed itinerary; proof that the expenses were paid for directly
(meaning the travel agent's underlying records, if the agent paid
for the tickets and rooms) and not reimbursed to the official;
a detailed agenda of the meetings, including who was there
and the topics discussed; as well as some record that filled in
the other details that would be relevant to company-sponsored
travel for an official. For example:

- Does the record adequately explain the use of all of the
  official's time?

- What was done between meetings?
- Did the official eat? With whom, and where?
- Should there be additional records somewhere that explain these things?
- If the official traveled with people from the company, what do those people's expense reimbursement requests look like?

Often the answer to the last question will reveal any lavish entertainment that might have occurred. If several people are submitting receipts from the same bar on the same night, that may be because they wanted to break up the costs among their different reimbursement requests to conceal the totality of the costs.

Asking and answering these kinds of questions can go a long way toward ensuring better records are kept. The truth of the matter is that most of these kinds of expenses are legitimate but poorly documented. But otherwise legitimate expenses that lack proper support still cause books and records problems.

Overall, you should have records that contain a complete explanation for the expenses and do not leave questions open and unasked. To properly resolve the questions raised by *Schering-Plough*, you need to be able to answer in the affirmative to the question: Based on what I know about how legitimate business is conducted, does this documentation tell a complete story and explain everything I need to know to understand this expense?

Consulting Arrangements

Like the issues just discussed, consultants received a chapter of their own. When it comes to third-party consultants and agents, documentation is critical. At the outset of any third-party relationship, proper documentation is your best defense against problems down the road. Your diligence file and your initial contracts define your relationship, your rights, and your remedies for all that comes later. Good documentation on the front end can save you down the road.

In Chapter 8, I discussed at length the problems of knowing who your third parties are and understanding what they are doing. Ensuring that the relationship is properly vetted and established is primarily an internal controls issue. Here the primary concern is how to ensure that the records you keep as your relationship progresses satisfy the FCPA's record-keeping requirements. And, much more like the *Schering-Plough* case, payments to intermediaries add a level of difficulty to the documentation process because you have less ability to explain or control what your agent does on your behalf.

Your contract with any third party should specify a level of detail required in invoices as well as the level of supporting documentation required. Invoices with cryptic descriptions such as "For services rendered" generally are not acceptable. How can you credibly claim to know what your agent is doing when there is effectively no descriptive record of it? Similarly, generic categories such as "miscellaneous" expenses should also be avoided. You want to think about the records from your consultants in the most cynical light.

Ask yourself how you would explain the charges on an invoice to someone who was predisposed to assume that the transaction was corrupt. Do the descriptions on the invoices make sense on their face—both the type of work or goods and the prices? Or do they require you to ask a lot of follow-up questions to ensure that you really understand what goods or services were provided? It is certainly true that you might need some technical expertise to understand a particular invoice, but if you ask the people in your company who have that expertise to explain what the line items on the invoices are for, can they do it? If they cannot, your documentation is not clear enough.

This level of inquiry strikes people as daunting, but it really is not. The vast majority of your expenditures make perfect sense, and the invoices for those expenditures are clear. The key to ensuring proper books and records is educating your accounting staff to focus on the areas of highest risk and to ask informed, practical questions about the documentation put before them. When it comes to consultants, you want the record to clearly reflect a genuine, legitimate arrangement for real services. You want a record that shows the services were preformed, the rates were reasonable, and the amounts you paid make sense in light of what was done. You can always send an invoice back to your consultants and say you are not paying it until they put more detail on it.

Trade Associations and Industry Groups

Many companies belong to trade associations and industry groups. In certain circumstances—such as when you are entering a new market—membership is almost required. There may be no other way to get to know the players in your industry and, therefore, no other way to gain any meaningful market share.

But membership in these groups often results in sizable payments that are difficult to explain and poorly documented. There are membership fees, payments to sponsor events, and often contributions made for specific causes the association has decided to support. To make matters worse, these organizations are often populated by government officials, especially in developing countries, or have members who are officials by virtue of being employees of state-owned entities.

The whole point of the membership in the association is to grow your business, so the payments to the association are made to "obtain or retain" business as that phrase is used in the FCPA. The question you have to wrestle with then is whether those payments are going to or benefiting an official. More to the point: Is the documentation of those payments sufficient to ward off a *Schering-Plough* analysis?

Although the trade association may well be a legitimate industry organization, that fact did nothing to protect *Schering-Plough* when it made payments to an indisputably legitimate charity. Remember that the essence of *Schering-Plough* is that recording the expense as a donation failed to capture the entire picture—the motive behind the donations was to curry favor with the official. The same could easily be said if you sponsored an association event at a resort where notable officials in the relevant industry were going to be flown in and put up for the weekend by the association. Sure, the sponsorship fee was paid to the association, but the purpose of the payment, *at least in part*, was to cover the travel, lodging, and entertainment costs of officials who, almost by definition, you are trying to influence. How will it look if you win business or receive a beneficial regulatory ruling a few months later over which that official could have exerted some influence? Even if you had no such intention, the corporate records may suggest a different story and be hard to explain away.

To the extent possible, you want to anticipate these problems so they can be addressed on the front end. The documentation of the expenses, including sponsorships and other one-time expenses, can be properly characterized to minimize after-the-fact criticisms and questions. Also, you want to make sure you have a complete diligence file about the association that includes what membership gives the company, who the other members are, and who sits on the committees that manage the association.

Seminars and Training Events

Seminars and training events present a range of documentation problems we have discussed in prior chapters. They

171

combine numerous risk factors, from vague (and potentially false) invoices from hotels or travel agencies, to the engagement of relevant government officials as guest speakers, to the basic problem of inviting employees of state-owned customers to attend. You will want your accounting staff to pay particular attention to expenses relating to these events. The more detail the better, and always be on guard for particular expenses that seem too high and could reflect manipulation of costs to conceal a slush fund.

Knowing Mischaracterizations

The recent *Natco* case contains an interesting twist on the books and records problem that ties back into the prior chapter's discussion of extortion. A Kazakhstan subsidiary of Houston-based oil and gas equipment maker Natco Group, Inc. was faced with two audits by Kazakhstan immigration prosecutors who claimed that Natco's expatriate employees did not have the required work visas. In each instance, the immigration prosecutors threatened fines, jail time, and deportation if the subsidiary did not pay a cash fine directly to the prosecutors.

Interestingly, in the SEC's cease-and-desist order against Natco, the SEC describes the cash payments as "extorted immigration fines." In the same vein, the SEC goes on to say that the subsidiary made the payments to the prosecutors "[b]elieving the prosecutor's threats to be genuine." Having negotiated these same documents with the SEC myself, I can tell you that phrases like those do not end up in these documents by accident. A fair reading is that the SEC may well have recognized that the immigration prosecutor's allegations were bogus and the threats to essentially shut down the business by jailing or deporting the employees amounted to extortion of the company.

But the SEC goes on to point out that the employees paid the "fines" out of their own pockets and then sought reimbursement from the company. The company—knowing full well what the payments were for—reimbursed the employees, but booked one of the reimbursements as a "payroll advance" and the other as "visa fines." Although "visa fines" is at least close to an accurate description, "payroll advance" clearly is not, and the company knew it was not at the time it booked it. For this, the SEC held Natco in violation of the FCPA's books and records provisions.

Based on the SEC's description of the payments as "extorted," it seems reasonably clear that the SEC probably did not view the payments as violations of the FCPA's anti-bribery provisions. The fact that the DOJ brought no action in the case certainly suggests that it did not see the payments as criminal in nature. Yet there was an obviously deliberate attempt to conceal the nature of what were very likely lawful payments. This is yet another example of the cover-up being worse than the crime (especially when there was no crime at all!).

The bottom line is that fake documents result in books and records violations even if what is being concealed is not an FCPA violation at all—indeed, even if the underlying expense was most likely *entirely legal*. False documentation is always a problem in its own right, and where the company explicitly condones the false recording of a transaction, you can almost guarantee that the U.S. government will not let it slide.

It is arguable that the SEC and DOJ took pity on Natco in this instance. As you may recall from Chapter 2, willful—that is, intentional—books and records violations can be criminally prosecuted. You can go to jail for up to 20 years, and a company can be fined up to $25,000,000 per violation. By those terms, the $65,000 fine Natco paid was a bargain (although it undoubtedly spent much, much more investigating the issues).

Fake Documentation

There is obviously a big difference between inadequate or ambiguous documentation and wholly fabricated documentation. Fake documents of the kind discussed in Chapter 5 are unacceptable in any legitimate business and will violate the FCPA.

The truth of the matter is that fake documents are hard to detect and hard to protect against. Any employee who is determined to commit an act of fraud through the use of fake documents can probably get away with it, especially if it is only an infrequently used strategy. The lengths to which some employees will go can be astounding. This is a point best illustrated with a story:

Once upon a time in the third world, a major company bought a much smaller company. As one would expect, it sent its internal auditors in to review the acquired company's books shortly after the acquisition closed. Minor issues were noted, but overall, the target was given a clean bill of health. A few months later, the regional finance manager came into work to find a handful of pages clipped together on her chair. Included in the packet were photocopies of several company checks made out to an individual, along with a photocopy of that individual's government-issued identification card that showed the recipient to be a government official.

Upon investigation, the transactions reflected in the documents were not found anywhere in the subsidiary's books. What they found instead were other checks with the same check numbers, purchase orders that matched the dates, amounts, and purchase order numbers but reflected mundane corporate expenses. Something was wrong. Either the company's books had been altered or the documents left with the regional manager were themselves fakes. The documents in the books looked just like they should—just like real checks, real purchase orders—and everything appeared to be booked properly.

But a forensic analysis of backed-up accounting data revealed a wholesale deception orchestrated by the target's general manager. Although the checks and purchase orders in the books were extremely well done fakes, the general manager had failed to consider that the original electronic accounting entries, made when the original transactions were booked, still existed on computer backup tapes that had been set aside in the normal course of business. There the original entries remained preserved despite the great efforts later undertaken to later conceal them. By comparing the historical backup data to the data as it existed at the time of the investigation, dozens of problematic transactions were uncovered.

As it turned out, the general manager knew that an internal audit would be coming after the acquisition. He also knew that he had engaged in many corrupt transactions that would not be viewed favorably by his new employer. So, the week before internal audit arrived, he had key members of the accounting staff stay late and replace the old transactions with new ones that would raise no questions. He even went so far as to go to existing vendors and pay them to fabricate documents for him. He provided dates, amounts, and purchase order numbers so that the fake transactions could be dropped into the books as exact replacements for the original transactions. And because he was buying them from legitimate outside vendors, the new records came with all of the seals and stamps required in that country. They were perfect fakes because they were, in some sense, real.

These things really happen in the world. They can happen anywhere, in any organization. The efforts people will go through go to conceal their wrongdoing can be astounding. Telling yourself that it cannot happen in your business is just self-deception. Telling yourself that your company's processes will catch things like this places too much faith in your processes. Employees—especially those with any real power or authority—will be able to get away with bad acts if that is what they are determined to do.

I tell this story to assuage some of your concerns. As a manager, you might be asking yourself what you could possibly do to stop something like that from happening in your organization. The answer is: probably nothing. If you genuinely have a rogue employee who takes steps to deceive you and conceal information (whether about bribery, fraud, or embezzlement), that employee will probably get away with it. You will end up with books and records that are inaccurate (or fabricated), and you may well have a host of other problems, too.

But if you have strong internal controls in place that were designed to stop this kind of behavior, at least you will have a good story to tell. Indeed, the more extraordinary the lengths to which employees have to go to hide their tracks, the better the defense you and your company have. Ironically, it acts as proof, in a way, of how strong your internal controls are if an employee has to go to great effort to circumvent them. But that's only *if* your internal controls are strong.

Which leads to our next topic.

What Are Internal Controls?

Internal controls are policies, procedures, monitoring, and training that are designed to ensure that company assets are used properly, with proper approval, and that transactions are properly recorded in the books and records. While it is theoretically possible to have good controls but bad books and records (and vice versa), the two generally go hand in hand—where there are record-keeping violations, an internal controls failure is almost presumed because the records would have been accurate had the controls been adequate.

Think of internal controls as an interrelated set of compliance mechanisms, all intended either to stop violations from occurring or to detect them as soon as possible once they do. Designing them is a specialty all its own, and I won't delve into the minutiae here. At the highest level, they consist of five concepts:

1. You should assess the risks associated with your business. Generally, this process is undertaken by compliance experts, both internally and with the help of outside consultants. But as a manager, you are closest to the ground. You actually see the business operating, and you need to be watchful for risk areas that might not be addressed adequately by the internal controls. This is especially true when your business is entering a new market. There may be local cultural or structural issues that your internal controls do not contemplate. For example, your human resources (HR) policies may require all employees to be paid by direct deposit, and your accounting policies may place a limit on the amount of cash that can be kept on hand. But in many developing countries, some employees may not have bank accounts (and may not be able to open them) and therefore must be paid in cash. Not only does this require an exemption from the HR policy, it also likely requires you to have more cash on hand than generally permitted in order to meet your payroll. But the presence of large amounts of cash creates new risks, for bribery, embezzlement, fraud, and a whole range of other problems. These are the kinds of issues you need to spot and resolve with your compliance department, to protect yourself and the company. After all, who is ultimately on the hook for any missing cash when your internal auditors come through?

2. You should have a comprehensive set of corporate policies and a corporate code of conduct that tells employees what rules they must follow to be an employee in good standing. This should go without saying, but I am often surprised how many companies do not have their policies translated into all of the local languages where they do business. If employees can't read them, they can't follow them. If your company can invest in opening a business in a particular country, it can afford to spend the modest sum required to get its policies translated into the local language. The failure to do so sends the wrong message and looks bad if you ever come under regulatory scrutiny.

3. You should have a set of procedures in place—ideally written procedures—that tell employees how to comply with the policies. Although some procedures may be set out in the general policy statements, many others may be department specific and relate to all of the mundane tasks that must be done in the ordinary course of business: what steps must be taken, what documents kept, what notices sent, approvals received, documents retained, and on and on. There is an art to figuring out the right level of detail, where employees need to be able to exercise their own judgment, and who has authority to deviate from or modify the procedures. And, just like your policies, your procedures need to be translated.

4. You should have a training program in place to ensure that employees understand the policies, procedures, regulations, and laws applicable to them. Ideally, the training will consist of formal and informal methods. To begin with, the policies should be widely distributed to and easily accessible by the employees. The Internet has made this much easier to do. Not long ago "corporate policies" were often treated as secret documents that were placed in a binder in the legal department accessible only by certain employees. If your company still operates that way, you should rethink your approach. If employees

cannot access the policies, it is unreasonable to think they can comply with them.

More important, though, is that many times the policies and procedures are voluminous. If employees read them when they start at the company, many may be forgotten or misremembered by the time employees actually need to apply them. Periodic training reinforces the policies and procedures. It also sends the message to employees that the company takes its policies seriously and genuinely expects compliance. It sends a similar message to government regulators if you ever have a compliance issue. If you take the time to periodically train and retrain your employees, it becomes harder for your company to be criticized for failing to enforce its own policies. For this reason, it is important to keep good records of training sessions, including the materials used and sign-in sheets that will prove who attended.

5. You should monitor compliance. I see an all-too-common fact pattern: A company develops a comprehensive compliance system but then fails to follow it. Having systemic violations of your own policies and procedures is one of the worst situations a company can have. The U.S. government can take the position that the mere existence of the policies demonstrates that the company knows that behavior that contradicts them is wrong or illegal. This puts the corporation and its management in a tough spot where they are viewed as either knowingly and intentionally allowing violations to occur or being so incompetent that they simply have no idea what is going on inside the business. As a legal matter, it is generally better to be seen as incompetent than criminal, but neither will do much for your career. The whole point of this book is to make you competent so you will never be accused of anything criminal.

A final case-in-point on this topic is the 2010 DOJ and SEC settlements with French engineering and construction firm

Technip S.A. The *Technip* matter involved numerous different transactions and resulted in total penalties and disgorgement of $338 million. But for our purposes here, it is language in the SEC's *Technip* complaint that is of most interest. The SEC took Technip to task for failing to implement adequate internal controls after it went public in the United States in August 2001. Focusing specifically on its procedures for due diligence of third parties, the SEC said:

> *The due diligence procedures adopted by Technip only required that potential agents respond to a written questionnaire, seeking minimal background information about the agent. No additional due diligence was required, such as an interview of the agent, or a background check, or obtaining information beyond that provided by the answers to the questionnaire. A senior executive of Technip admitted that the due diligence procedures adopted by Technip were a perfunctory exercise, conducted so that Technip would have some documentation in its files of purported due diligence.*

The takeaway is that for your internal controls to be taken seriously, they have to be more than window dressing. A compliance program that exists solely to ensure that you have something in your files, but that is in no way designed to dig into and check the legitimacy of transactions and information, will not be given the level of credit you want. A good compliance program can yield great benefit to you and your company, but a bad one can be turned against you.

Good Records and Controls Can Keep You Out of Jail

This book ends with a discussion of the U.S. Sentencing Guidelines and the ways in which good compliance really can keep the government off your back, but here I offer a brief mention of a new statute that proves this point.

The United Kingdom recently enacted a new anti-bribery law that, although untested, is far more draconian than the FCPA. By and large, it covers all of the situations discussed in this book but does not permit facilitating payments and vastly extends potential criminal liability for companies.

Indeed, the new U.K. Bribery Act imposes criminal liability on companies for *negligently* failing to prevent acts of bribery by its employees or agents. This is a big deal and essentially means that conduct that would not be an anti-bribery violation at all under the FCPA (after all, it is not a crime under the FCPA to be incompetent you must have the required level of intent) is criminalized under U.K. law. That means that incompetence *is* criminalized under the U.K. Bribery Act.

But even this harsh new U.K. law places an emphasis on compliance. Indeed, the act provides a complete defense to a criminal charge where a company can show that it had an adequate system of internal controls in place to stop acts of bribery—even if the system ultimately fails.

The law does not require perfection; it merely requires a serious effort. Thus, although the U.K. Bribery Act contains much harsher penalties than the FCPA for the same conduct, it also contains the best defense in the world. What an adequate system of internal controls will look like under the U.K. law is not yet settled, but I would be willing to bet it will look a lot like what I describe in this book. Although the FCPA does not provide a complete defense for compliance efforts, as discussed in Chapter 12, a comprehensive set of internal controls still has significant benefits under U.S. law.

CHAPTER 11

Are You Buying a Problem?
Due Diligence in Acquisitions and Government Contracts

All of the issues discussed in this book can exist in any international business, which means they can exist in any company that your company may consider buying. But think of how little you really know about any business you acquire. Even in the best of circumstances, where you can ask for and get any information you request in the due diligence process, you probably won't be able to get down to the level of detail necessary to detect many of the issues discussed in this book.

This fact creates serious risk regardless of whether the acquisition target was subject to the FCPA before the acquisition. Where the target was already subject to the act, you may well acquire all of its liabilities right along with its assets, including FCPA liabilities for transactions that occurred perhaps years before. If the target was not subject to the FCPA—a situation that is in many ways worse—you may become liable for any ongoing transactions, contracts, or business practices that violate the FCPA the instant the deal closes, even though your company did not participate in them and knows nothing about them.

Acquirers have a tendency to focus on the material aspects of a target (the big product lines, the high-value assets, or particular intellectual property or geographic dominance that have strategic meaning for the acquirer) and view everything else as just detail. This may be the correct view from a purely financial or strategic perspective. After all, the thinking goes, even if that small subsidiary in the Philippines, Morocco, India, or wherever is completely messed up, it is so small that it is *not material* to the overall deal. Even if you shut it down and take a total loss on that portion of the business, it simply won't matter.

But FCPA and other corruption problems in those remote outposts can significantly impact the overall business, resulting in major liabilities, disruptions, distractions, and damage. This can be especially true if those problems are allowed to continue, unchecked, long after the acquisition. The failure to pay attention to those remote subsidiaries goes right to the heart of the internal controls discussion from Chapter 10. Failure to pay attention is a failure of internal controls.

Tag, You're It: How Other People's Problems Become Yours

When it comes to FCPA due diligence, the first thing you need to ask yourself is: How risky is this deal? That risk assessment dictates the level of diligence required. Generally, your company will have lawyers helping with this process who are well versed in the FCPA and know the right questions to ask. But your lawyers can only work with the information provided to them. Being in the same industry, you may well be in a position to know if the target company is misleading you or omitting something critical. Are they saying they have no government customers when you know that they have a joint venture that does significant government business? Do they say that they do not use any third-party consultants when you know they use the same sales agent that you use in a particular country?

When you are doing a deal, your lawyers will likely have FCPA diligence checklists and questionnaires that will seek specific information from the target relating to FCPA risk factors (essentially all of which have been discussed at length in this book). The discovery of FCPA issues in the acquisition target does not automatically derail an acquisition, but it can disrupt or delay it. We'll discuss a few high-profile examples next and then walk through the kind of planning you should undertake to ensure a quick and sufficient postacquisition remediation of any FCPA risks.

We discussed the *InVision* case in Chapters 4 and 6. You may recall that InVision sold explosive detection systems to airports in Thailand, the Philippines, and China through foreign sales agents. The sales agents sought to influence the relevant purchasing personnel at various government-controlled airports in those countries by offering gifts, travel, and cash. The discovery of this activity took place in the context of a merger, whereby General Electric (GE) was to purchase InVision.

As a result of discovering this activity during the merger process, the merger was delayed for approximately a year. During this time, InVision undertook a thorough investigation, made a voluntary disclosure to the SEC and DOJ, and ultimately negotiated a resolution with both agencies. In the end, GE still purchased the company after InVision had resolved the matter.

Other companies are not so lucky. After Lockheed Martin Corporation announced that it would buy Titan Corporation in 2003, the parties began the normal premerger due diligence process. During that process, Titan learned, among other things, that between 1999 and 2001, it had funneled more than $3.5 million through an agent in Benin, Africa, who was the personal business advisor to the country's president. A substantial portion of the money went toward the president's reelection campaign. The ultimate goal behind the payments was to help Titan develop a telecommunications project in Benin and to increase its management fee for that project. The payments themselves were booked as "consulting services" through false invoices, and the money was paid in small increments to avoid drawing attention to them. By this point in this book, you should easily recognize all of the signs of FCPA problems exhibited by this series of transactions.

But unlike GE in the *InVision* deal, Lockheed backed out of its purchase of Titan. Indeed, Lockheed had been the subject of a prior FCPA action in the 1990s that was, at the time, the largest FCPA case in history. Lockheed may well have wanted to avoid any involvement with a company tainted by FCPA issues.

Although GE's acquisition of InVision was delayed for a year, such a delay can be advantageous because problems can be dealt with while they still reside solely within the target. If the problems turn out to be substantial, you would rather know that before you purchase the company. Indeed, the problems may well affect the purchase price if they are substantial enough. As discussed in the next section, it may not always be practical (or even possible) to wait, but knowing as much as you can about any potential liabilities you might acquire is generally preferable.

The consequences can transcend mere FCPA liability to the U.S. government. For example, the failed merger not only left Titan in a lurch, it also resulted in an ominous legal development that ties directly back into the *InVision* case. When the SEC announced its settlement in *Titan*, it also issued a report of investigation aimed at providing guidance to other securities issuers. In its report, the SEC noted that the Lockheed/Titan merger agreement had been attached to a proxy statement filed with the SEC in connection with the planned merger. The agreement contained a representation by Titan that:

> *to the knowledge of the Company, neither the Company nor any of its Subsidiaries, nor any director, officer, agent or Employee of the Company or any of its subsidiaries, has ...*

taken any action which would cause the Company or any of its Subsidiaries to be in violation of the Foreign Corrupt Practices Act.[1]

The SEC noted that, after the internal investigation revealed Titan's FCPA problems, Titan knew that its prior representation was no longer accurate. Yet Titan did not go back and amend or correct this filing. The SEC further noted that failure to correct such a false and misleading statement (even though not contained in a formal disclosure document) could provide the basis for an enforcement action for securities fraud.

This was the exact theory used by class action plaintiffs in a securities fraud suit arising from the *InVision* matter. Although that lawsuit failed for various technical reasons, the United States Court of Appeals that ruled on that case found that lawsuits could be brought based on false representations made in the merger agreements attached to securities filings. All of which means that companies should think very hard about the representations made in merger and other documents filed with the SEC because statements in those documents may be rendered false by information uncovered later during the diligence process.

Although all of these problems can arise on the way toward an acquisition, more often than not they are not uncovered until after the acquisition, when you have a chance to access all of the details of the business you now own. When problems start to crop up, they are now *your* problems, not someone else's. While it is true that these inherited problems are not of your own making, the law does not explicitly allow for a window of time to correct them—although the faster you do so, the more lenient

---

[1]See Titan Report of Investigation, SEC Release No. 51283, available at: www.sec.gov/litigation/investreport/34-51238.htm.

the SEC and DOJ are likely to be. Companies often ask "How long do we have?" or "What is the grace period for cleaning things up?" That fact is, there is no grace period, but there are some guidelines you can use to place your company in the best possible position.

The *Halliburton* Opinion

In 2008, Halliburton was faced with a difficult decision. It wanted to buy a U.K. company in the oil services business that operated in more than 50 countries, many of them high-corruption countries. The problem was that the target company had already received an unconditional bid from a consortium of primarily foreign investors. Under U.K. law, Halliburton had to submit its competing bid very quickly (which did not allow for meaningful FCPA due diligence) and, in any event, it was not entitled to receive any FCPA (or any other) diligence material that the other bidder had not also received. The other bidder, being a non-U.S. consortium, had received very little in the way of FCPA diligence materials. At the end of the day, Halliburton had to bid on an oil services company, doing business in high-corruption countries in a high-corruption industry, completely blind.

Understandably, Halliburton was concerned about inheriting liabilities.

Halliburton sought a formal opinion from the DOJ regarding its potential FCPA exposure in the event it acquired the target without conducting any FCPA due diligence and then discovered ongoing FCPA violations. Although the resulting DOJ opinion does not provide binding precedent (and few companies are likely to find themselves in the identical circumstance), the parameters set out in the opinion provide a very good window into the DOJ's aggressive enforcement stance.

In its request for the opinion, Halliburton put forward a plan to address the FCPA risks caused by the acquisition. The DOJ approved the plan and stated that, if the plan was followed, it would not bring any enforcement action based on any pre-acquisition FCPA violations or any postacquisition violations that occurred within the target during *the first six months* following the acquisition, so long as these conditions were met:

- No Halliburton personnel knowingly played any role in approving or making the payments at issue.
- All pre- and postacquisition violations were fully disclosed to the DOJ.
- All violations were stopped within six months of the acquisition.

Although the DOJ allowed for the possibility that some areas might take longer than six months to investigate and that some violations might not be able to be stopped within the six-month window, any extension of the six-month period would be solely at the DOJ's discretion.

While this effectively gave Halliburton a very narrow six-month window in which the FCPA could be violated by the target, you should not assume that you and your company will have a similar window. The plan Halliburton put forth is aggressive, and the DOJ emphasized that the situation was unique because Halliburton did not have a meaningful opportunity to conduct pre-acquisition due diligence.

Because most companies will have at least some opportunity for due diligence, they can expect less accommodation from the U.S. government than Halliburton got. Meaning that the Halliburton plan, or something like it, is probably the *minimum* a company can do if it expects to get the DOJ and SEC to have mercy on it for postacquisition problems it discovers. Other factors could come into play to garner more sympathy with the U.S. government, such as the acquired company taking steps to falsify records and conceal illegal activity. But such factors occur on a case-by-case basis and cannot form part of a meaningful plan of action for dealing with acquired businesses.

To understand the level of compliance commitment expected of you and your company after an acquisition, let's look at the diligence process Halliburton agreed to undertake.

First off, Halliburton committed to develop a comprehensive, risk-based due diligence work plan within 10 days of closing. The plan was to address all of the major FCPA risk categories: the use of agents and other third parties; commercial dealings with state-owned customers; joint ventures and other similar arrangements; customs and immigration matters; tax matters; and any government licenses and permits. The strategy employed was to rank these various areas in terms of high, medium, and low risk and then proceed to tackle each category on separate but concurrent timelines.

There is an element of artificiality to the rankings, in the sense that any of these areas could be the source of significant problems, or no problems at all. Furthermore, much of the necessary work, in terms of data collection and analysis, will be the same regardless of the rankings. But setting aside the pragmatic issues surrounding the implementation of such a plan, the plan itself was aggressive and comprehensive. Halliburton agreed to have initial results of its high-risk analysis within 90 days of closing, and its medium- and low-risk analyses within 120 and 180 days respectively. For issues requiring more than 180 days to review, the DOJ allowed for extra time but required consistent progress reports. But the outer limit set for the completion of the entire review was one year from the closing date.

Second, Halliburton committed to engage appropriate outside counsel experienced in FCPA matters, as well as third-party consultants such as forensic accountants, to conduct the work. Although an allowance was made for using internal resources "as appropriate," the main takeaway was that the U.S. government appeared to think little of the ability of nonspecialized internal people to conduct the kind of diligence expected. Bottom line: The process was going to be expensive. Not only because of the required use of outside FCPA experts, but because it was to be carried out in "all appropriate locations," meaning that on-site work would have to be done to talk to local employees and examine the local records. Furthermore, the plan specified review of emails and accounting documents, which is often labor intensive and requires further outside expertise and resources.

The takeaway is that you must provide sufficient resources for the diligence process your company undertakes before and after an acquisition for it to be meaningful. A company cannot hope to pinch pennies—by not engaging experts, not harvesting and reviewing email and other electronic documents, not traveling to the actual overseas office locations to interview employees and review records—and expect the process to be accorded any respect by the U.S. government. A genuine commitment to FCPA compliance, the DOJ seems to be signaling, will be underscored by a meaningful commitment of resources. It is unrealistic for a company to expect to acquire a multinational business and then spend no time or resources to ensure that the business actually complies with U.S. law. Failure to devote these resources likely means that the company will be held accountable for any and all violations that occur after the acquisition, without any leniency. After all, a failure to take any steps to seek out and stop such violations exhibits a lack of seriousness about compliance. Why would the DOJ or SEC want to reward that?

Third, all third parties that continued doing business with the acquired company after Halliburton's acquisition were expected to sign new contracts. The plan was clear that these would not be modifications of existing contracts but entirely new contracts that incorporated FCPA representations and warranties as well as other anti-corruption provisions, including audit rights over the third party's books and records. Although this portion of the plan was limited to circumstances where the new contracts were "appropriate," it is not clear to what length Halliburton was expected to go in pressing for new contracts.

As a practical matter, there are many circumstances where an acquiring company has no right to demand new contracts. In other circumstances, there may be an ability to get a new contract in place, but the third party might have commercial leverage that would require the acquirer to give up something valuable in return for the new agreement. It is an open question how far the acquirer has to go on this issue, but obviously a real, provable effort should be undertaken.

Fourth, Halliburton had to immediately impose its Code of Conduct and FCPA policies, procedures, and internal controls on the target. Furthermore, it had to provide FCPA and anti-corruption training to all of the acquired company's officers and relevant employees, which included all management, sales, accounting, and financial control personnel (indeed, the same audience who will generally be reading this book) within 60 days of the acquisition. Given that the target did business in 50 countries, this was a tremendous burden—essentially training a country a day from the date of acquisition forward.

Finally, Halliburton committed to keeping the target a wholly owned subsidiary for so long as the DOJ continued to investigate. Halliburton agreed that the target (and its officers, directors, employees, agents, subsidiaries, and affiliates) would remain liable for any past or future FCPA violations. This is perhaps the central part of the plan for understanding just how aggressive the DOJ is in these cases.

After undertaking all of the work just set out, Halliburton was only protecting itself. No such protections were afforded to the company it wanted to buy. Halliburton had to undertake an intense review, all over the world, and then hand over the results of that review to the DOJ. The DOJ agreed not to pursue Halliburton for any bad acts uncovered during the review but retained the right to pursue the wholly owned subsidiary. That subsidiary, its key personnel, and its significant business lines were still potentially subject to massive exposure if the review uncovered major problems.

Let me be clear here: Halliburton, the corporate parent, had managed to protect itself from being tainted by the acquired company, but the acquired company remained on the hook. From Halliburton's standpoint, this was a great outcome because it was not at risk for some of the more onerous penalties that can accompany FCPA convictions, such as debarment from government contracts. But from an overall organizational perspective, all of the exposure still remained—it was just localized within the wholly owned subsidiary Halliburton acquired. But, of course, significant fiscal damage to that entity would have an overall effect on the consolidated corporate financials. Any hit to the bottom line would ultimately be a hit to Halliburton's bottom line.

In the end, there is no panacea that can cure the effects of historical FCPA violations. Due diligence, properly done both pre- and postacquisition can help reduce the risks of someone else's problems tainting your company, but it is not necessarily a get-out-of-jail-free card. Ideally, you want a strong due diligence component as part of your overall package of internal controls. Something that says: *We don't buy a business without doing this set of procedures before the acquisition and this other set of procedures right after acquisition.* Having a serious diligence program dovetails with your overall compliance program by ensuring that your newly acquired businesses and employees are properly trained, educated, and brought into the fold where their actions can be subjected to the company's overarching compliance mechanism.

Because, ultimately, it is that mechanism that saves you. It trains people not to violate the FCPA, it stops violations before they occur, it finds them when they do occur, it permits for remedial actions once violations are found, and it documents everything so that you can prove to anyone who asks what an excellent job your company does at ferreting out these very obscure and often well-hidden violations.

A Note on Joint Ventures

Although not a third-party transaction in the strictest sense, and not an acquisition either, joint ventures present similar issues. Your joint venture partners need to undergo a similar diligence process. This is especially true where your company will own more than 50 percent of the resulting JV. When you control the JV, the acts of your partner will be attributed to you just as the acts of an agent would. But even where you are a minority partner, you will want to have a solid diligence file. Indeed, the FCPA explicitly requires a company owning 50 percent or less of a business to "use its influence, to the extent reasonable . . . to cause [the business] to devise and maintain a system of internal accounting controls" consistent with the FCPA.

CHAPTER 12

Time Off for Good Behavior
Why Compliance Matters

We have now walked though all of the major FCPA risk areas in great detail. We have also discussed policies, procedures, internal controls, record-keeping issues, and due diligence procedures all aimed and keeping these violations out of your organization. Here we are now at the final chapter, which poses the ultimate question: Why should you care?

At the outset, we discussed the large fines many companies have faced in recent years. We also discussed individuals being criminally prosecuted and going to jail with ever-increasing frequency and for significant periods of time. We also examined the *Technip* settlement, where the SEC took the company to task for failing to have internal controls that did anything more than accepting the answers provided by third parties without subjecting them to any independent confirmation or scrutiny. And on the other end of the spectrum, we read about how Halliburton promised to move mountains and expend huge resources on a diligence process that ultimately did not shield the overall corporate group from financial exposure. After all this, you may be left thinking that there is just no point to working so hard to stop FCPA violations when all it takes is a few bad apples in your company to spoil the whole effort.

Not so fast. Good compliance programs have significant benefits if you ever find yourself in the middle of an FCPA investigation.

Ultimately, this book is about keeping both you and your company out of trouble. The single best way to do that is to ensure that your company has the best compliance program possible. Your job is to understand the risk areas and to be vigilant in policing those risk areas. As I have said many times throughout this book, no compliance program is perfect and no manager is perfect. You will have failures. You will have rogue employees or agents who, no matter what you do, are going to violate your policies and the FCPA. The way you protect yourself is through your compliance program, which will allow you to credibly say that you did everything you could and you should not be held responsible. Believe it or not, this is an approach that really does work—especially for individual managers.

There are three ways compliance programs can keep you and your company out of trouble or, at minimum, limit the damage from a criminal violation.

1. Foremost is the fact that good compliance programs result in compliance with the law. If your program is effective at preventing illegal conduct, you are in the best possible position.
2. If illegal conduct occurs despite the existence of a good compliance program, the existence of the program can affect the U.S. government's charging decision. It may result in a complete declination or a decision to pursue some lesser charge than could have been pursued.
3. If the company is prosecuted, a good corporate compliance program will be factored into the sentencing analysis set out in the United States Federal Sentencing Guidelines. Under these guidelines, a good compliance program

(combined with demonstrable compliance efforts) can substantially reduce a recommended sentence.

Good Compliance Programs Affect Charging Decisions

The DOJ has a policy statement known as the Principles of Federal Prosecution of Business Organizations (Principles) that is revised from time to time and incorporated into the U.S. Attorneys' Manual, which is binding on all DOJ prosecutors. The purpose of the Principles is to guide prosecutorial decisions about whether to charge a corporation with a crime or negotiate a plea, and the severity of the punishment that should be sought.

The Principles set out nine factors that "prosecutors should consider ... in reaching a decision as to the proper treatment of a corporate target." One of those factors is "the corporation's remedial actions, including any efforts to implement an effective corporate compliance program or to improve an existing one, to replace responsible management, to discipline or terminate wrongdoers, to pay restitution, and to cooperate with relevant government agencies."[1]

This single factor captures much of what has been discussed in this book. You may recall Chapter 2's discussion of the dynamics of internal investigations. There I described the interrelated pressure points of:

1. Potential personal liability for corporate directors and officers.
2. The beneficial effect of self-reporting to and cooperation with the U.S. government.
3. How those often combine and motivate companies to toss lower-level employees out in the cold for the greater good of the company.

---

[1]See full text of the Principles in Appendix 2.

Here the DOJ's explicit policy on corporate charging decisions mandates consideration of those very concepts:

- Has the company disciplined or terminated wrongdoers?
- Has the company cooperated with relevant agencies?
- Does the company have an "effective corporate compliance program" in place?

The Principles then go on to describe "critical factors in evaluating" compliance programs. They begin by noting that "no compliance program can ever prevent all criminal activity by a corporation's employees" and that perfection is not required. What is essential is a determination of "whether the program is adequately designed for maximum effectiveness in preventing and detecting wrongdoing by employees and whether corporate management is enforcing the program or is tacitly encouraging or pressuring employees to engage in misconduct to achieve business objectives."

In assessing whether a compliance program is well designed and whether the tone at the top of the company is sufficiently serious about compliance, prosecutors are directed to consider these factors:

- The comprehensiveness of the compliance program.
- The extent and pervasiveness of the criminal misconduct.
- The number and level of the corporate employees involved.
- The seriousness, duration, and frequency of the misconduct.
- Any remedial actions taken by the corporation including, for example, disciplinary action against past violators uncovered by the prior compliance program, and revisions to corporate compliance programs in light of lessons learned.
- The promptness of any disclosure of wrongdoing to the government.

Once again, all of the factors previously discussed are here:

- How comprehensive is the program?
- How bad was the conduct, and who was involved?
- How serious were the violations?
- What did the company do once the violation was uncovered?

Disciplinary action and disclosure to the U.S. government are explicitly mentioned. And, as a practical matter, once the bad conduct has occurred, revising the compliance policy, disciplining the employees, and reporting to the DOJ and SEC are the only factors the company actually has control over, so you can easily understand how important these factors become.

In addition, prosecutors can also consider whether a company's directors exercise independent review over corporate actions (rather than simply approving whatever is put before them), whether there is direct reporting of timely information to the board, and whether sufficient staff and resources have been devoted to the program to allow it to be effective. These issues go to the level of commitment the organization has to compliance, but, as with most of the other factors, little can be done to change the historical facts once violations are uncovered. A commitment to improving these things after a violation is discovered is helpful, but the only fully *prospective* actions a company can take to improve its position as a crisis unfolds relate to investigating the wrongdoing, taking disciplinary action against employees, and cooperating with the U.S. government.

Essentially, prosecutors are asked to ascertain whether the compliance program is merely a "paper program" or whether it reflects a sincere and earnest effort to achieve compliance, in terms of oversight, resources, and sufficient reaction to compliance issues when they arise. The more serious the program, the response to wrongdoing, and the level of cooperation, the more lenient a prosecutor is likely to be.

Good Compliance Programs Reduce Sentences

The Sentencing Guidelines—the relevant parts of which are included as Appendix 3 to this book—set out a much more elaborate, but conceptually similar, framework for determining the recommended penalty for every violation of every federal criminal law. They generally take into account various aggravating and mitigating factors that can increase or reduce the recommended sentence. The main provision applicable to this book comes from the guideline on sentencing "organizations." The Sentencing Guidelines explicitly take into account whether you have an "effective compliance and ethics program" (as well as other factors) when calculating what is known as the culpability score—that is, when determining how guilty you are. Not surprisingly, the better your program, the less culpable you are.

It is important to understand how the Sentencing Guidelines address compliance programs because they are the U.S. government's clearest statement about what it thinks compliance programs should do and how they should do it. Thematically, there is nothing new here, but I think walking through the topics the Sentencing Guidelines emphasize is helpful to show you just how coherent they really are.

At the highest level, the Sentencing Guidelines set out two overarching goals for compliance programs:

1. The company must "exercise due diligence to prevent and detect criminal conduct."
2. The company's compliance policy must "promote an organizational culture that encourages ethical conduct and a commitment to compliance with the law."

Just like the Principles of Federal Prosecution of Business Organizations, the Sentencing Guidelines go on to note that your compliance program does not have to be perfect at stopping all criminal violations. The Sentencing Guidelines require vigilance and a program that is "generally effective." Indeed, the Sentencing Guidelines explicitly state that the "failure to prevent or detect" a particular violation "does not necessarily mean that the program is not generally effective in preventing and detecting criminal conduct." Which means you can fail sometimes. You do not have to be perfect. You just have to be serious and committed. As I have said before, if employees take great pains to circumvent your company's controls and conceal their activity, the Sentencing Guidelines do not automatically assume your compliance program is insufficient.

The Sentencing Guidelines include a list of what is considered the minimum requirements for an effective compliance program:

- Clearly articulated policies and procedures against FCPA violations (as well as other laws) designed to prevent and detect criminal conduct.
- Senior management and the board of directors must be knowledgeable about the compliance program and exercise reasonable oversight over it.
- Assignment of responsibility for the compliance and ethics program to specific high-level personnel within the company, including the responsibility to develop and implement the processes and procedures.
- These responsible individuals must be given adequate resources, appropriate authority, and direct access to the board of directors.
- The company should exclude those with a history of criminal activity from positions of compliance authority. In other words, you want to take reasonable efforts to keep the fox from guarding the henhouse. Run background checks on the people you are putting in charge of compliance program, even if you're certain they are Boy or Girl Scouts.

- The company must keep employees informed of and trained on the relevant laws, regulations, policies, and procedures. This training should extend all the way from the board of directors down through senior management, middle management, all company employees, and even agents and third parties the company uses, where it is reasonable to do so.
- The company should routinely monitor and audit its compliance program to detect any criminal conduct and to ensure the compliance program is working.
- The company needs to have and to publicize a reporting system that includes mechanisms that allow anonymous or confidential reporting of policy violations or criminal conduct, or where an employee can seek guidance on compliance without fear of retaliation.
- The compliance program has to be consistently enforced throughout the company, including incentives to encourage compliance and disciplinary measures for failing to comply or, in the case of managers, failing to take reasonable steps to ensure compliance by others.
- The company must take "reasonable steps" to respond appropriately to the discovery of criminal activity by reacting in a manner designed to prevent further similar criminal conduct, including making modifications to the compliance program, if necessary. "Reasonable steps" is defined to include self-reporting to or cooperating with enforcement authorities "where appropriate."
- The company must undertake periodic reassessments of its compliance program and modify it accordingly where weaknesses are detected.

Importantly, if high-level personnel are found to be involved in the criminal conduct—which is often the case in FCPA matters—this fact does not automatically disqualify the compliance program from consideration, but it does trigger four additional requirements for the compliance program to reduce the company's culpability. As a practical matter, then, these additional requirements are almost mandatory if a company is going to derive sentencing benefit from the most serious criminal violations (which, because of their seriousness, will almost always involve high-level personnel). These are:

1. The individuals responsible for the compliance program must have a direct reporting line to the company's governing authority—typically the board or audit committee. This effectively means a serious commitment to compliance will require the head of the compliance program to be a senior officer of the company.

2. The compliance program must have discovered the violation before it is discovered outside the company or before discovery outside the company was reasonably likely. This means you won't get credit if someone beats you to the government (or the media) with the information, even if the DOJ or SEC has not reached out to you.

3. The company must promptly report the violation to the U.S. government. This effectively mandates voluntary disclosure to the DOJ and SEC for any violations involving high-level company personnel if you want to take advantage of the culpability credit in any resulting sentencing analysis. This can be a difficult problem because an internal investigation may go on for quite some time before a company is even aware that high-level personnel were involved in a violation. The existence of the investigation itself could complicate matters because it increases the likelihood that someone else who learns of the investigation might beat you to the government—meaning your compliance program may be disqualified under item 2.

4. The individuals in charge of the compliance program cannot themselves be involved in or willfully blind to the violation.

It is also worth noting that what constitutes an ethical culture is not necessarily defined by external norms of behavior. If you happen to operate in an industry that has taken it upon itself to adopt informal industry guidelines—the pharmaceutical industry comes to mind—the failure to adhere to those industry standards could also reflect poorly on your compliance program. The Sentencing Guidelines specifically allow for this consideration as well.

There are a lot of other specifics in the Sentencing Guidelines, and there are many additional factors that compliance professionals will incorporate into any plan they design. But in general, they all follow the themes discussed throughout this book: Design and implement a good plan, give the right high-level people in the company the necessary authority and resources to implement the plan, train your people, monitor and audit their compliance, take action where violations occur (including disciplinary action and voluntary reporting to the U.S. government), and revise your policies and procedures as necessary. Seems simple enough, right?

Of course it is not. As with any major initiative, there are organizational and logistical difficulties in implementing robust compliance programs. When problems occur, there is a tendency to focus on the immediate or to not want to make a big deal out of something that may seem like an inconsequential issue at first. As an individual manager, you may feel that compliance issues are someone else's problem because you have a business or department to run. But you should resist this tendency. The easiest way to ensure that you do not get crosswise with an investigation within your company is to take compliance seriously.

The overall goal of the Sentencing Guidelines is clear. Your compliance program should "promote an organizational culture that encourages ethical conduct and a commitment to compliance with the law." Protecting yourself by displaying a commitment to these ideals should not eat up much of your time and should not be a distraction. You need to be able to see issues in your organization—which is the whole point of this book—and then display the right attitude about them by reporting them to the right people.

It is precisely this level of seriousness that the U.S. government will try to pin down when weighing what degree of penalty to levy on you or your company. The Sentencing Guidelines summarize themselves in this manner:

> *The requirements set forth in this guideline are intended to achieve reasonable prevention and detection of criminal conduct for which the organization would be vicariously liable. The prior diligence of an organization in seeking to prevent and detect criminal conduct has a direct bearing on the appropriate penalties and probation terms for the organization if it is convicted and sentenced for a criminal offense.*

The same can be said of individual managers. The harder you have tried to stop FCPA violations, the more lenient the authorities will be when you have a violation. You don't have to be perfect, just persistent.

And it is not just with the SEC and DOJ that good compliance matters. As I have mentioned elsewhere, plaintiffs' lawyers are scrambling to find a good method for suing companies for securities fraud when they violate the FCPA. A direct quote from a Delaware Chancery Court opinion in a case involving Dow Chemical illustrates the power a good program has in insulating companies (and their directors and officers) from securities fraud liability. In *Dow Chemical*, the court said:

> *Plaintiffs cannot meet their burden here for another reason. The Dow board has set up policies to prevent improper dealing with third parties. In particular, Dow's Code of Ethics expressly prohibits any unethical payments to third*

*parties. . . . Plaintiffs cannot simultaneously argue that the
Dow board "utterly failed" to meet its oversight duties yet had
"corporate governance procedures" in place without alleging
that the board deliberately failed to monitor its ethics policy
or its internal procedures.*[2]

Thus, having a good compliance policy raises the bar for
plaintiffs who want to allege mismanagement or unethical conduct by the company. Obviously, it is much harder to prove
"deliberate" disregard for policies and procedures than it is to
prove a failure of adequate oversight and mismanagement by
not having a compliance program at all.

Having good compliance policies and procedures, then, can
not only help by reducing exposure to the federal government,
it can also reduce potential civil liability. After all, whether it
is a federal criminal indictment, a securities class action lawsuit, or a derivative action (as *Dow Chemical* was), everyone
who comes after your company will have to show a bad state
of mind—either intent to commit an act or at least willful disregard for the law or recklessness—and a serious compliance
program (with all of the monitoring and follow-up a serious
program requires) makes such a showing extremely difficult.
A good compliance program demonstrates that a company is
doing everything it can to *comply* with the law, not to violate it.

In an overt recognition of this basic fact, the new U.K.
Bribery Act discussed in Chapter 10 takes the unusual step of
imposing criminal liability for negligently failing to prevent an
act of bribery. For reasons we will not get into here, this is a his-
toric expansion of criminal liability that should have people up
in arms. But perhaps the reason there is not panic in the streets
is that the U.K. Bribery Act provides a very simple and sensible

---

[2]See *In re Dow Chemical Co. Derivative Litigation*, No. 4348-CC (Del.
Chanc. Ct. 2010) for the full decision.

route to avoid criminal liability: It provides a complete defense for any company that has an adequate compliance program.

And that is why compliance matters.

The DOJ and SEC may not give FCPA violations quite the get-out-of-jail-free card that the U.K. Bribery Act does, but serious, effective FCPA compliance programs still offer tremendous protections under the Principles of Federal Prosecution of Business Organizations and the U.S. Sentencing Guidelines. And that is what this entire book has been about: protecting you and your company through knowledge of the FCPA and the many real-world ways violations can creep into your business.

* * *

I'll end where I began.

I have seen careers ruined that should not have been. Well-intentioned managers who found themselves in difficult situations, in unfamiliar cultures, who either failed to see FCPA issues at all or failed to take them seriously when they did. Most managers never intend to do anything illegal, and I believe that most people truly want to do the right thing.

When I began this book two years ago on a flight to Indonesia, my goal was to give managers the knowledge they needed to see potential FCPA problems and stop them. Or, failing that, to see them and protect themselves by raising the issues to people above them in their companies so they would be protected if things went wrong. I'm now finishing up the final edits on a flight from Chicago to Beijing, and little has changed in my world of seemingly endless FCPA issues.

My sincere hope is that no one who reads this book will ever run afoul of the FCPA. That is surely too much to ask, but it is good to have goals.

Aaron G. Murphy
Somewhere over China
August 2010

Compliance Certificate

I, _____, hereby certify the following:

1. That I have read the book *Foreign Corrupt Practice Act: A Practical Resource for Managers and Executives* and that I understand its contents;

2. That I understand the prohibitions of the United States Foreign Corrupt Practices Act of 1977 (FCPA);

3. That I have raised any questions that I have about FCPA compliance to my supervisors or other relevant personnel within the company and have had them adequately addressed;

4. That I have not violated, or approved or condoned violations of, the FCPA;

5. That any FCPA issues or violations of which I am aware have been reported to my supervisors or other relevant personnel within the company; and,

6. That to the best of my knowledge the employees who report to me are familiar with and have complied with the FCPA.

_____

Signature

_____

Print Name and Title

_____

Date

Anti-Bribery, Record-Keeping, and Internal Controls Provisions of the Foreign Corrupt Practices Act*

15 U.S.C.§78m. Periodical and Other Reports

(a) Reports by issuer of security; contents

Every issuer of a security registered pursuant to section 78l of this title shall file with the Commission, in accordance with such rules and regulations as the Commission may prescribe as necessary or appropriate for the proper protection of investors and to insure fair dealing in the security—

(1) such information and documents (and such copies thereof) as the Commission shall require to keep reasonably current the information and documents required to be included in or filed with an application or registration statement filed

---

*Current through Pub. L. 105-366 (November 10, 1998)

pursuant to section 78l of this title, except that the Commission may not require the filing of any material contract wholly executed before July 1, 1962.

(2) such annual reports (and such copies thereof), certified if required by the rules and regulations of the Commission by independent public accountants, and such quarterly reports (and such copies thereof), as the Commission may prescribe.

Every issuer of a security registered on a national securities exchange shall also file a duplicate original of such information, documents, and reports with the exchange.

(b) Form of report; books, records, and internal accounting; directives

* * *

(2) Every issuer which has a class of securities registered pursuant to section 78l of this title and every issuer which is required to file reports pursuant to section 78o(d) of this title shall—

(A) make and keep books, records, and accounts, which, in reasonable detail, accurately and fairly reflect the transactions and dispositions of the assets of the issuer; and

(B) devise and maintain a system of internal accounting controls sufficient to provide reasonable assurances that–

(i) transactions are executed in accordance with management's general or specific authorization;

(ii) transactions are recorded as necessary (I) to permit preparation of financial statements in conformity with generally accepted accounting principles or any other criteria applicable to such statements, and (II) to maintain accountability for assets;

    (iii) access to assets is permitted only in accordance with management's general or specific authorization; and

    (iv) the recorded accountability for assets is compared with the existing assets at reasonable intervals and appropriate action is taken with respect to any differences.

(3)(A) With respect to matters concerning the national security of the United States, no duty or liability under paragraph (2) of this subsection shall be imposed upon any person acting in cooperation with the head of any Federal department or agency responsible for such matters if such act in cooperation with such head of a department or agency was done upon the specific, written directive of the head of such department or agency pursuant to Presidential authority to issue such directives. Each directive issued under this paragraph shall set forth the specific facts and circumstances with respect to which the provisions of this paragraph are to be invoked. Each such directive shall, unless renewed in writing, expire one year after the date of issuance.

(B) Each head of a Federal department or agency of the United States who issues such a directive pursuant to this paragraph shall maintain a complete file of all such directives and shall, on October 1 of each year, transmit a summary of matters covered by such directives in force at any time during the previous year to the Permanent Select Committee on Intelligence of the House of Representatives and the Select Committee on Intelligence of the Senate.

(4) No criminal liability shall be imposed for failing to comply with the requirements of paragraph (2) of this subsection except as provided in paragraph (5) of this subsection.

(5) No person shall knowingly circumvent or knowingly fail to implement a system of internal accounting controls or knowingly falsify any book, record, or account described in paragraph (2).

(6) Where an issuer which has a class of securities registered pursuant to section 78l of this title or an issuer which is required to file reports pursuant to section 78o(d) of this title holds 50 per centum or less of the voting power with respect to a domestic or foreign firm, the provisions of paragraph (2) require only that the issuer proceed in good faith to use its influence, to the extent reasonable under the issuer's circumstances, to cause such domestic or foreign firm to devise and maintain a system of internal accounting controls consistent with paragraph (2). Such circumstances include the relative degree of the issuer's ownership of the domestic or foreign firm and the laws and practices governing the business operations of the country in which such firm is located. An issuer which demonstrates good faith efforts to use such influence shall be conclusively presumed to have complied with the requirements of paragraph (2).

(7) For the purpose of paragraph (2) of this subsection, the terms "reasonable assurances" and "reasonable detail" mean such level of detail and degree of assurance as would satisfy prudent officials in the conduct of their own affairs.

* * *

15 U.S.C.§78dd-1 [Section 30A of the Securities & Exchange Act of 1934]

Prohibited Foreign Trade Practices by Issuers

(a) Prohibition

It shall be unlawful for any issuer which has a class of securities registered pursuant to section 78l of this title or which is required to file reports under section 78o(d) of this title, or for any officer, director, employee, or agent of such issuer or any stockholder thereof acting on behalf of such issuer, to make use of the mails or any means or instrumentality of interstate commerce corruptly in furtherance of an offer, payment, promise to pay, or authorization of the payment of any money, or offer, gift, promise to give, or authorization of the giving of anything of value to—

(1) any foreign official for purposes of—
    (A) (i) influencing any act or decision of such foreign official in his official capacity, (ii) inducing such foreign official to do or omit to do any act in violation of the lawful duty of such official, or (iii) securing any improper advantage; or
    (B) inducing such foreign official to use his influence with a foreign government or instrumentality thereof to affect or influence any act or decision of such government or instrumentality,

in order to assist such issuer in obtaining or retaining business for or with, or directing business to, any person;

(2) any foreign political party or official thereof or any candidate for foreign political office for purposes of—
    (A) (i) influencing any act or decision of such party, official, or candidate in its or his official capacity, (ii) inducing such party, official, or candidate to do or omit to do an act in violation of the lawful duty of such party, official, or candidate, or (iii) securing any improper advantage; or
    (B) inducing such party, official, or candidate to use its or his influence with a foreign government or instrumentality thereof to affect or influence any act or decision of such government or instrumentality.

in order to assist such issuer in obtaining or retaining business for or with, or directing business to, any person; or

(3) any person, while knowing that all or a portion of such money or thing of value will be offered, given, or promised, directly or indirectly, to any foreign official, to any foreign political party or official thereof, or to any candidate for foreign political office, for purposes of—

   (A) (i) influencing any act or decision of such foreign official, political party, party official, or candidate in his or its official capacity, (ii) inducing such foreign official, political party, party official, or candidate to do or omit to do any act in violation of the lawful duty of such foreign official, political party, party official, or candidate, or (iii) securing any improper advantage; or

   (B) inducing such foreign official, political party, party official, or candidate to use his or its influence with a foreign government or instrumentality thereof to affect or influence any act or decision of such government or instrumentality,

   in order to assist such issuer in obtaining or retaining business for or with, or directing business to, any person.

(b) Exception for routine governmental action

Subsections (a) and (g) of this section shall not apply to any facilitating or expediting payment to a foreign official, political party, or party official the purpose of which is to expedite or to secure the performance of a routine governmental action by a foreign official, political party, or party official.

(c) Affirmative defenses

It shall be an affirmative defense to actions under subsection (a) or (g) of this section that—

(1) the payment, gift, offer, or promise of anything of value that was made, was lawful under the written laws and regulations of the foreign official's, political party's, party official's, or candidate's country; or

(2) the payment, gift, offer, or promise of anything of value that was made, was a reasonable and bona fide expenditure, such as travel and lodging expenses, incurred by or on behalf of a foreign official, party, party official, or candidate and was directly related to—

   (A) the promotion, demonstration, or explanation of products or services; or

   (B) the execution or performance of a contract with a foreign government or agency thereof.

(d) Guidelines by Attorney General

Not later than one year after August 23, 1988, the Attorney General, after consultation with the Commission, the Secretary of Commerce, the United States Trade Representative, the Secretary of State, and the Secretary of the Treasury, and after obtaining the views of all interested persons through public notice and comment procedures, shall determine to what extent compliance with this section would be enhanced and the business community would be assisted by further clarification of the preceding provisions of this section and may, based on such determination and to the extent necessary and appropriate, issue—

   (1) guidelines describing specific types of conduct, associated with common types of export sales arrangements and business contracts, which for purposes of the Department of Justice's present enforcement policy, the Attorney General determines would be in conformance with the preceding provisions of this section; and

   (2) general precautionary procedures which issuers may use on a voluntary basis to conform their conduct to the Department of Justice's present enforcement policy regarding the preceding provisions of this section.

The Attorney General shall issue the guidelines and procedures referred to in the preceding sentence in accordance with the provisions of subchapter II of chapter 5 of Title 5 and those guidelines and procedures shall be subject to the provisions of chapter 7 of that title.

(e) Opinions of Attorney General

(1) The Attorney General, after consultation with appropriate departments and agencies of the United States and after obtaining the views of all interested persons through public notice and comment procedures, shall establish a procedure to provide responses to specific inquiries by issuers concerning conformance of their conduct with the Department of Justice's present enforcement policy regarding the preceding provisions of this section. The Attorney General shall, within 30 days after receiving such a request, issue an opinion in response to that request. The opinion shall state whether or not certain specified prospective conduct would, for purposes of the Department of Justice's present enforcement policy, violate the preceding provisions of this section. Additional requests for opinions may be filed with the Attorney General regarding other specified prospective conduct that is beyond the scope of conduct specified in previous requests. In any action brought under the applicable provisions of this section, there shall be a rebuttable presumption that conduct, which is specified in a request by an issuer and for which the Attorney General has issued an opinion that such conduct is in conformity with the Department of Justice's present enforcement policy, is in compliance with the preceding provisions of this section. Such a presumption may be rebutted by a preponderance of the evidence. In considering the presumption for purposes of this paragraph, a court shall weight all relevant factors, including but not limited to whether the information submitted to the

Attorney General was accurate and complete and whether it was within the scope of the conduct specified in any request received by the Attorney General. The Attorney General shall establish the procedure required by this paragraph in accordance with the provisions of subchapter II of chapter 5 of Title 5 and that procedure shall be subject to the provisions of chapter 7 of that title.

(2) Any document or other material which is provided to, received by, or prepared in the Department of Justice or any other department or agency of the United States in connection with a request by an issuer under the procedure established under paragraph (1), shall be exempt from disclosure under section 552 of Title 5 and shall not, except with the consent of the issuer, be made publicly available, regardless of whether the Attorney General responds to such a request or the issuer withdraws such request before receiving a response.

(3) Any issuer who has made a request to the Attorney General under paragraph (1) may withdraw such request prior to the time the Attorney General issues an opinion in response to such request. Any request so withdrawn shall have no force or effect.

(4) The Attorney General shall, to the maximum extent practicable, provide timely guidance concerning the Department of Justice's present enforcement policy with respect to the preceding provisions of this section to potential exporters and small businesses that are unable to obtain specialized counsel on issues pertaining to such provisions. Such guidance shall be limited to responses to requests under paragraph (1) concerning conformity of specified prospective conduct with the Department of Justice's present enforcement policy regarding the preceding provisions of this section and general explanations of compliance

responsibilities and of potential liabilities under the preceding provisions of this section.

(f) Definitions

For purposes of this section:

(1)(A) The term "foreign official" means any officer or employee of a foreign government or any department, agency, or instrumentality thereof, or of a public international organization, or any person acting in an official capacity for or on behalf of any such government or department, agency, or instrumentality, or for or on behalf of any such public international organization.

(B) For purposes of subparagraph (A), the term "public international organization" means—

(i) an organization that is designated by Executive Order pursuant to section 1 of the International Organizations Immunities Act (22 U.S.C. §288); or

(ii) any other international organization that is designated by the President by Executive order for the purposes of this section, effective as of the date of publication of such order in the Federal Register.

(2)(A) A person's state of mind is "knowing" with respect to conduct, a circumstance, or a result if—

(i) such person is aware that such person is engaging in such conduct, that such circumstance exists, or that such result is substantially certain to occur; or

(ii) such person has a firm belief that such circumstance exists or that such result is substantially certain to occur.

(B) When knowledge of the existence of a particular circumstance is required for an offense, such knowledge is established if a person is aware of a high probability of the existence of such circumstance, unless the person actually believes that such circumstance does not exist.

(3)(A) The term "routine governmental action" means only an action which is ordinarily and commonly performed by a foreign official in—

   (i) obtaining permits, licenses, or other official documents to qualify a person to do business in a foreign country;

   (ii) processing governmental papers, such as visas and work orders;

   (iii) providing police protection, mail pick-up and delivery, or scheduling inspections associated with contract performance or inspections related to transit of goods across country;

   (iv) providing phone service, power and water supply, loading and unloading cargo, or protecting perishable products or commodities from deterioration; or

   (v) actions of a similar nature.

(B) The term "routine governmental action" does not include any decision by a foreign official whether, or on what terms, to award new business to or to continue business with a particular party, or any action taken by a foreign official involved in the decision-making process to encourage a decision to award new business to or continue business with a particular party.

(g) Alternative Jurisdiction

(1) It shall also be unlawful for any issuer organized under the laws of the United States, or a State, territory, possession, or commonwealth of the United States or a political subdivision thereof and which has a class of securities registered

pursuant to section 12 of this title or which is required to file reports under section 15(d) of this title, or for any United States person that is an officer, director, employee, or agent of such issuer or a stockholder thereof acting on behalf of such issuer, to corruptly do any act outside the United States in furtherance of an offer, payment, promise to pay, or authorization of the payment of any money, or offer, gift, promise to give, or authorization of the giving of anything of value to any of the persons or entities set forth in paragraphs (1), (2), and (3) of this subsection (a) of this section for the purposes set forth therein, irrespective of whether such issuer or such officer, director, employee, agent, or stockholder makes use of the mails or any means or instrumentality of interstate commerce in furtherance of such offer, gift, payment, promise, or authorization.

(2) As used in this subsection, the term "United States person" means a national of the United States (as defined in section 101 of the Immigration and Nationality Act (8 U.S.C. §1101)) or any corporation, partnership, association, joint-stock company, business trust, unincorporated organization, or sole proprietorship organized under the laws of the United States or any State, territory, possession, or commonwealth of the United States, or any political subdivision thereof.

15 U.S.C.§78dd-2. Prohibited Foreign Trade Practices by Domestic Concerns

(a) Prohibition

It shall be unlawful for any domestic concern, other than an issuer which is subject to section 78dd-1 of this title, or for any officer, director, employee, or agent of such domestic concern or any stockholder thereof acting on behalf of such domestic concern, to make use of the mails or any means or instrumentality of interstate commerce corruptly in furtherance of an offer, payment, promise to pay, or authorization of the payment of any money, or offer, gift, promise to give, or authorization of the giving of anything of value to—

(1) any foreign official for purposes of—
    (A) influencing any act or decision of such foreign official in his official capacity, (ii) inducing such foreign official to do or omit to do any act in violation of the lawful duty of such official, or (iii) securing any improper advantage; or
    (B) inducing such foreign official to use his influence with a foreign government or instrumentality thereof to affect or influence any act or decision of such government or instrumentality,
    in order to assist such domestic concern in obtaining or retaining business for or with, or directing business to, any person;
(2) any foreign political party or official thereof or any candidate for foreign political office for purposes of—
    (A) influencing any act or decision of such party, official, or candidate in its or his official capacity, (ii) inducing such party, official, or candidate to do or omit to do an act in violation of the lawful duty of such party, official, or candidate, or (iii) securing any improper advantage; or
    (B) inducing such party, official, or candidate to use its or his influence with a foreign government or instrumentality thereof to affect or influence any act or decision of such government or instrumentality,
    in order to assist such domestic concern in obtaining or retaining business for or with, or directing business to, any person;

(3) any person, while knowing that all or a portion of such money or thing of value will be offered, given, or promised, directly or indirectly, to any foreign official, to any foreign political party or official thereof, or to any candidate for foreign political office, for purposes of—

(A) influencing any act or decision of such foreign official, political party, party official, or candidate in his or its official capacity, (ii) inducing such foreign official, political party, party official, or candidate to do or omit to do any act in violation of the lawful duty of such foreign official, political party, party official, or candidate, or (iii) securing any improper advantage; or

(B) inducing such foreign official, political party, party official, or candidate to use his or its influence with a foreign government or instrumentality thereof to affect or influence any act or decision of such government or instrumentality,

in order to assist such domestic concern in obtaining or retaining business for or with, or directing business to, any person.

(b) Exception for routine governmental action

Subsections (a) and (i) of this section shall not apply to any facilitating or expediting payment to a foreign official, political party, or party official the purpose of which is to expedite or to secure the performance of a routine governmental action by a foreign official, political party, or party official.

(c) Affirmative defenses

It shall be an affirmative defense to actions under subsection (a) or (i) of this section that—

(1) the payment, gift, offer, or promise of anything of value that was made, was lawful under the written laws and

regulations of the foreign official's, political party's, party official's, or candidate's country; or

(2) the payment, gift, offer, or promise of anything of value that was made, was a reasonable and bona fide expenditure, such as travel and lodging expenses, incurred by or on behalf of a foreign official, party, party official, or candidate and was directly related to–
   (A) the promotion, demonstration, or explanation of products or services; or
   (B) the execution or performance of a contract with a foreign government or agency thereof.

(d) Injunctive relief

(1) When it appears to the Attorney General that any domestic concern to which this section applies, or officer, director, employee, agent, or stockholder thereof, is engaged, or about to engage, in any act or practice constituting a violation of subsection (a) or (i) of this section, the Attorney General may, in his discretion, bring a civil action in an appropriate district court of the United States to enjoin such act or practice, and upon a proper showing, a permanent injunction or a temporary restraining order shall be granted without bond.

(2) For the purpose of any civil investigation which, in the opinion of the Attorney General, is necessary and proper to enforce this section, the Attorney General or his designee are empowered to administer oaths and affirmations, subpoena witnesses, take evidence, and require the production of any books, papers, or other documents which the Attorney General deems relevant or material to such investigation. The attendance of witnesses and the production of documentary evidence may be required from any place in the United States, or any territory, possession,

or commonwealth of the United States, at any designated place of hearing.

(3) In case of contumacy by, or refusal to obey a subpoena issued to, any person, the Attorney General may invoke the aid of any court of the United States within the jurisdiction of which such investigation or proceeding is carried on, or where such person resides or carries on business, in requiring the attendance and testimony of witnesses and the production of books, papers, or other documents. Any such court may issue an order requiring such person to appear before the Attorney General or his designee, there to produce records, if so ordered, or to give testimony touching the matter under investigation. Any failure to obey such order of the court may be punished by such court as a contempt thereof.

All process in any such case may be served in the judicial district in which such person resides or may be found. The Attorney General may make such rules relating to civil investigations as may be necessary or appropriate to implement the provisions of this subsection.

(e) Guidelines by Attorney General

Not later than 6 months after August 23, 1988, the Attorney General, after consultation with the Securities and Exchange Commission, the Secretary of Commerce, the United States Trade Representative, the Secretary of State, and the Secretary of the Treasury, and after obtaining the views of all interested persons through public notice and comment procedures, shall determine to what extent compliance with this section would be enhanced and the business community would be assisted by further clarification of the preceding provisions of this section and may, based on such determination and to the extent necessary and appropriate, issue—

(1) guidelines describing specific types of conduct, associated with common types of export sales arrangements and business contracts, which for purposes of the Department of Justice's present enforcement policy, the Attorney General determines would be in conformance with the preceding provisions of this section; and

(2) general precautionary procedures which domestic concerns may use on a voluntary basis to conform their conduct to the Department of Justice's present enforcement policy regarding the preceding provisions of this section.

The Attorney General shall issue the guidelines and procedures referred to in the preceding sentence in accordance with the provisions of subchapter II of chapter 5 of Title 5 and those guidelines and procedures shall be subject to the provisions of chapter 7 of that title.

(f) Opinions of Attorney General

(1) The Attorney General, after consultation with appropriate departments and agencies of the United States and after obtaining the views of all interested persons through public notice and comment procedures, shall establish a procedure to provide responses to specific inquiries by domestic concerns concerning conformance of their conduct with the Department of Justice's present enforcement policy regarding the preceding provisions of this section. The Attorney General shall, within 30 days after receiving such a request, issue an opinion in response to that request. The opinion shall state whether or not certain specified prospective conduct would, for purposes of the Department of Justice's present enforcement policy, violate the preceding provisions of this section. Additional requests for opinions may be filed with the Attorney

General regarding other specified prospective conduct that is beyond the scope of conduct specified in previous requests. In any action brought under the applicable provisions of this section, there shall be a rebuttable presumption that conduct, which is specified in a request by a domestic concern and for which the Attorney General has issued an opinion that such conduct is in conformity with the Department of Justice's present enforcement policy, is in compliance with the preceding provisions of this section. Such a presumption may be rebutted by a preponderance of the evidence. In considering the presumption for purposes of this paragraph, a court shall weigh all relevant factors, including but not limited to whether the information submitted to the Attorney General was accurate and complete and whether it was within the scope of the conduct specified in any request received by the Attorney General. The Attorney General shall establish the procedure required by this paragraph in accordance with the provisions of subchapter II of chapter 5 of Title 5 and that procedure shall be subject to the provisions of chapter 7 of that title.

(2) Any document or other material which is provided to, received by, or prepared in the Department of Justice or any other department or agency of the United States in connection with a request by a domestic concern under the procedure established under paragraph (1), shall be exempt from disclosure under section 552 of Title 5 and shall not, except with the consent of the domestic concern, by made publicly available, regardless of whether the Attorney General response to such a request or the domestic concern withdraws such request before receiving a response.

(3) Any domestic concern who has made a request to the Attorney General under paragraph (1) may withdraw such

request prior to the time the Attorney General issues an opinion in response to such request. Any request so withdrawn shall have no force or effect.

(4) The Attorney General shall, to the maximum extent practicable, provide timely guidance concerning the Department of Justice's present enforcement policy with respect to the preceding provisions of this section to potential exporters and small businesses that are unable to obtain specialized counsel on issues pertaining to such provisions. Such guidance shall be limited to responses to requests under paragraph (1) concerning conformity of specified prospective conduct with the Department of Justice's present enforcement policy regarding the preceding provisions of this section and general explanations of compliance responsibilities and of potential liabilities under the preceding provisions of this section.

(g) Penalties

(1)(A) Any domestic concern that is not a natural person and that violates subsection (a) or (i) of this section shall be fined not more than $2,000,000.

(B) Any domestic concern that is not a natural person and that violates subsection (a) or (i) of this section shall be subject to a civil penalty of not more than $10,000 imposed in an action brought by the Attorney General.

(2)(A) Any natural person that is an officer, director, employee, or agent of a domestic concern, or stockholder acting on behalf of such domestic concern, who willfully violates subsection (a) or (i) of this section shall be fined not more than $100,000 or imprisoned not more than 5 years, or both.

(B) Any natural person that is an officer, director, employee, or agent of a domestic concern, or stockholder acting on behalf of such domestic concern, who violates subsection (a) or (i) of this section shall be subject to a civil penalty of not more than $10,000 imposed in an action brought by the Attorney General.

(3) Whenever a fine is imposed under paragraph (2) upon any officer, director, employee, agent, or stockholder of a domestic concern, such fine may not be paid, directly or indirectly, by such domestic concern.

(h) Definitions

For purposes of this section:

(1) The term "domestic concern" means—

(A) any individual who is a citizen, national, or resident of the United States; and

(B) any corporation, partnership, association, joint-stock company, business trust, unincorporated organization, or sole proprietorship which has its principal place of business in the United States, or which is organized under the laws of a State of the United States or a territory, possession, or commonwealth of the United States.

(2)(A) The term "foreign official" means any officer or employee of a foreign government or any department, agency, or instrumentality thereof, or of a public international organization, or any person acting in an official capacity for or on behalf of any such government or department, agency, or instrumentality, or for or on behalf of any such public international organization.

(B) For purposes of subparagraph (A), the term "public international organization" means—

(i) an organization that has been designated by Executive order pursuant to Section 1 of the

International Organizations Immunities Act (22 U.S.C. §288); or

(ii) any other international organization that is designated by the President by Executive order for the purposes of this section, effective as of the date of publication of such order in the Federal Register.

(3)(A) A person's state of mind is "knowing" with respect to conduct, a circumstance, or a result if—

(i) such person is aware that such person is engaging in such conduct, that such circumstance exists, or that such result is substantially certain to occur; or

(ii) such person has a firm belief that such circumstance exists or that such result is substantially certain to occur.

(B) When knowledge of the existence of a particular circumstance is required for an offense, such knowledge is established if a person is aware of a high probability of the existence of such circumstance, unless the person actually believes that such circumstance does not exist.

(4)(A) The term "routine governmental action" means only an action which is ordinarily and commonly performed by a foreign official in—

(i) obtaining permits, licenses, or other official documents to qualify a person to do business in a foreign country;

(ii) processing governmental papers, such as visas and work orders;

(iii) providing police protection, mail pick-up and delivery, or scheduling inspections associated with contract performance or inspections related to transit of goods across country;

(iv) providing phone service, power and water supply, loading and unloading cargo, or protecting perishable products or commodities from deterioration; or

(v) actions of a similar nature.

(B) The term "routine governmental action" does not include any decision by a foreign official whether, or on what terms, to award new business to or to continue business with a particular party, or any action taken by a foreign official involved in the decision-making process to encourage a decision to award new business to or continue business with a particular party.

(5) The term "interstate commerce" means trade, commerce, transportation, or communication among the several States, or between any foreign country and any State or between any State and any place or ship outside thereof, and such term includes the intrastate use of—

(A) a telephone or other interstate means of communication, or

(B) any other interstate instrumentality.

(i) Alternative jurisdiction

(1) It shall also be unlawful for any United States person to corruptly do any act outside the United States in furtherance of an offer, payment, promise to pay, or authorization of the payment of any money, or offer, gift, promise to give, or authorization of the giving of anything of value to any of the persons or entities set forth in paragraphs (1), (2), and (3) of subsection (a), for the purposes set forth therein, irrespective of whether such United States person makes use of the mails or any means or instrumentality of interstate commerce in furtherance of such offer, gift, payment, promise, or authorization.

(2) As used in this subsection, a "United States person" means a national of the United States (as defined in section 101 of the Immigration and Nationality Act (8 U.S.C. §1101)) or any corporation, partnership, association, joint-stock company, business trust, unincorporated organization, or sole proprietorship organized under the laws of the United States or any State, territory, possession, or commonwealth of the United States, or any political subdivision thereof.

15 U.S.C. §78dd-3. Prohibited Foreign Trade Practices by Persons Other Than Issuers or Domestic Concerns

(a) Prohibition

It shall be unlawful for any person other than an issuer that is subject to section 30A of the Securities Exchange Act of 1934 or a domestic concern, as defined in section 104 of this Act), or for any officer, director, employee, or agent of such person or any stockholder thereof acting on behalf of such person, while in the territory of the United States, corruptly to make use of the mails or any means or instrumentality of interstate commerce or to do any other act in furtherance of an offer, payment, promise to pay, or authorization of the payment of any money, or offer, gift, promise to give, or authorization of the giving of anything of value to—

(1) any foreign official for purposes of—
   (A) (i) influencing any act or decision of such foreign official in his official capacity, (ii) inducing such foreign official to do or omit to do any act in violation of the lawful duty of such official, or (iii) securing any improper advantage; or
   (B) inducing such foreign official to use his influence with a foreign government or instrumentality thereof to

affect or influence any act or decision of such government or instrumentality,

in order to assist such person in obtaining or retaining business for or with, or directing business to, any person;

(2) any foreign political party or official thereof or any candidate for foreign political office for purposes of—

(A) (i) influencing any act or decision of such party, official, or candidate in its or his official capacity, (ii) inducing such party, official, or candidate to do or omit to do an act in violation of the lawful duty of such party, official, or candidate, or (iii) securing any improper advantage; or

(B) inducing such party, official, or candidate to use its or his influence with a foreign government or instrumentality thereof to affect or influence any act or decision of such government or instrumentality.

in order to assist such person in obtaining or retaining business for or with, or directing business to, any person; or

(3) any person, while knowing that all or a portion of such money or thing of value will be offered, given, or promised, directly or indirectly, to any foreign official, to any foreign political party or official thereof, or to any candidate for foreign political office, for purposes of—

(A) (i) influencing any act or decision of such foreign official, political party, party official, or candidate in his or its official capacity, (ii) inducing such foreign official, political party, party official, or candidate to do or omit to do any act in violation of the lawful duty of such foreign official, political party, party official, or candidate, or (iii) securing any improper advantage; or

(B) inducing such foreign official, political party, party official, or candidate to use his or its influence with a foreign government or instrumentality thereof to affect or influence any act or decision of such government or instrumentality,

in order to assist such person in obtaining or retaining business for or with, or directing business to, any person.

(b) Exception for routine governmental action

Subsection (a) of this section shall not apply to any facilitating or expediting payment to a foreign official, political party, or party official the purpose of which is to expedite or to secure the performance of a routine governmental action by a foreign official, political party, or party official.

(c) Affirmative defenses

It shall be an affirmative defense to actions under subsection (a) of this section that–

(1) the payment, gift, offer, or promise of anything of value that was made, was lawful under the written laws and regulations of the foreign official's, political party's, party official's, or candidate's country; or

(2) the payment, gift, offer, or promise of anything of value that was made, was a reasonable and bona fide expenditure, such as travel and lodging expenses, incurred by or on behalf of a foreign official, party, party official, or candidate and was directly related to–

(A) the promotion, demonstration, or explanation of products or services; or

(B) the execution or performance of a contract with a foreign government or agency thereof.

(d) Injunctive relief

(1) When it appears to the Attorney General that any person to which this section applies, or officer, director, employee, agent, or stockholder thereof, is engaged, or about to engage, in any act or practice constituting a violation of subsection (a) of this section, the Attorney General may,

in his discretion, bring a civil action in an appropriate district court of the United States to enjoin such act or practice, and upon a proper showing, a permanent injunction or a temporary restraining order shall be granted without bond.

(2) For the purpose of any civil investigation which, in the opinion of the Attorney General, is necessary and proper to enforce this section, the Attorney General or his designee are empowered to administer oaths and affirmations, subpoena witnesses, take evidence, and require the production of any books, papers, or other documents which the Attorney General deems relevant or material to such investigation. The attendance of witnesses and the production of documentary evidence may be required from any place in the United States, or any territory, possession, or commonwealth of the United States, at any designated place of hearing.

(3) In case of contumacy by, or refusal to obey a subpoena issued to, any person, the Attorney General may invoke the aid of any court of the United States within the jurisdiction of which such investigation or proceeding is carried on, or where such person resides or carries on business, in requiring the attendance and testimony of witnesses and the production of books, papers, or other documents. Any such court may issue an order requiring such person to appear before the Attorney General or his designee, there to produce records, if so ordered, or to give testimony touching the matter under investigation. Any failure to obey such order of the court may be punished by such court as a contempt thereof.

(4) All process in any such case may be served in the judicial district in which such person resides or may be found. The Attorney General may make such rules relating to civil investigations as may be necessary or appropriate to implement the provisions of this subsection.

(e) Penalties

(1)(A) Any juridical person that violates subsection (a) of this section shall be fined not more than $2,000,000.

(B) Any juridical person that violates subsection (a) of this section shall be subject to a civil penalty of not more than $10,000 imposed in an action brought by the Attorney General.

(2)(A) Any natural person who willfully violates subsection (a) of this section shall be fined not more than $100,000 or imprisoned not more than 5 years, or both.

(B) Any natural person who violates subsection (a) of this section shall be subject to a civil penalty of not more than $10,000 imposed in an action brought by the Attorney General.

(3) Whenever a fine is imposed under paragraph (2) upon any officer, director, employee, agent, or stockholder of a person, such fine may not be paid, directly or indirectly, by such person.

(f) Definitions

For purposes of this section:

(1) The term "person," when referring to an offender, means any natural person other than a national of the United States (as defined in 8 U.S.C. §1101) or any corporation, partnership, association, joint-stock company, business trust, unincorporated organization, or sole proprietorship organized under the law of a foreign nation or a political subdivision thereof

(2) (A) The term "foreign official" means any officer or employee of a foreign government or any department, agency, or instrumentality thereof, or of a public international organization, or any person acting in an official

capacity for or on behalf of any such government or department, agency, or instrumentality, or for or on behalf of any such public international organization.

For purposes of subparagraph (A), the term "public international organization" means—

(i) an organization that has been designated by Executive Order pursuant to Section 1 of the International Organizations Immunities Act (22 U.S.C. §288); or

(ii) any other international organization that is designated by the President by Executive order for the purposes of this section, effective as of the date of publication of such order in the Federal Register.

(3)(A) A person's state of mind is "knowing" with respect to conduct, a circumstance, or a result if—

(i) such person is aware that such person is engaging in such conduct, that such circumstance exists, or that such result is substantially certain to occur; or

(ii) such person has a firm belief that such circumstance exists or that such result is substantially certain to occur.

(B) When knowledge of the existence of a particular circumstance is required for an offense, such knowledge is established if a person is aware of a high probability of the existence of such circumstance, unless the person actually believes that such circumstance does not exist.

(4)(A) The term "routine governmental action" means only an action which is ordinarily and commonly performed by a foreign official in—

(i) obtaining permits, licenses, or other official documents to qualify a person to do business in a foreign country;

(ii) processing governmental papers, such as visas and work orders;

(iii) providing police protection, mail pick-up and delivery, or scheduling inspections associated with contract performance or inspections related to transit of goods across country;

(iv) providing phone service, power and water supply, loading and unloading cargo, or protecting perishable products or commodities from deterioration; or

(v) actions of a similar nature.

(B) The term "routine governmental action" does not include any decision by a foreign official whether, or on what terms, to award new business to or to continue business with a particular party, or any action taken by a foreign official involved in the decision-making process to encourage a decision to award new business to or continue business with a particular party.

(5) The term "interstate commerce" means trade, commerce, transportation, or communication among the several States, or between any foreign country and any State or between any State and any place or ship outside thereof, and such term includes the intrastate use of—

(A) a telephone or other interstate means of communication, or

(B) any other interstate instrumentality.

15 U.S.C. §78ff. Penalties

(a) Willful violations; false and misleading statements

Any person who willfully violates any provision of this chapter (other than section 78dd-1 of this title), or any rule or regulation thereunder the violation of which is made unlawful or the observance of which is required under the terms of this chapter, or any person who willfully and knowingly makes, or causes to be made, any statement in any application, report, or document required to be filed under this chapter or any rule or regulation thereunder or any undertaking contained in a registration statement as provided in subsection (d) of section 78o of this title, or by any self-regulatory organization in connection with an application for membership or participation therein or to become associated with a member thereof, which statement was false or misleading with respect to any material fact, shall upon conviction be fined not more than $5,000,000, or imprisoned not more than 20 years, or both, except that when such person is a person other than a natural person, a fine not exceeding $25,000,000 may be imposed; but no person shall be subject to imprisonment under this section for the violation of any rule or regulation if he proves that he had no knowledge of such rule or regulation.

(b) Failure to file information, documents, or reports
Any issuer which fails to file information, documents, or reports required to be filed under subsection (d) of section 78o of this title or any rule or regulation thereunder shall forfeit to the United States the sum of $100 for each and every day such failure to file shall continue. Such forfeiture, which shall be in lieu of any criminal penalty for such failure to file which might be deemed to arise under subsection (a) of this section, shall be payable into the Treasury of the United States and shall be recoverable in a civil suit in the name of the United States.

(c) Violations by issuers, officers, directors, stockholders, employees, or agents of issuers

    (1)(A) Any issuer that violates subsection (a) or (g) of section 30A of this title [15 U.S.C. §78dd-1] shall be fined not more than $2,000,000.

(B) Any issuer that violates subsection (a) or (g) of section 30A of this title [15 U.S.C. §78dd-1] shall be subject to a civil penalty of not more than $10,000 imposed in an action brought by the Commission.

(2)(A) Any officer, director, employee, or agent of an issuer, or stockholder acting on behalf of such issuer, who willfully violates subsection (a) or (g) of section 30A of this title [15 U.S.C. §78dd-1] shall be fined not more than $100,000, or imprisoned not more than 5 years, or both.

(B) Any officer, director, employee, or agent of an issuer, or stockholder acting on behalf of such issuer, who violates subsection (a) or (g) of section 30A of this title [15 U.S.C. §78dd-1] shall be subject to a civil penalty of not more than $10,000 imposed in an action brought by the Commission.

(3) Whenever a fine is imposed under paragraph (2) upon any officer, director, employee, agent, or stockholder of an issuer, such fine may not be paid, directly or indirectly, by such issuer.

Relevant Provisions of the Principles of Federal Prosecution of Business Organizations

United States Attorneys Manual Section 9-28.800

Corporate Compliance Programs

General Principle: Compliance programs are established by corporate management to prevent and detect misconduct and to ensure that corporate activities are conducted in accordance with applicable criminal and civil laws, regulations, and rules. The Department encourages such corporate self-policing, including voluntary disclosures to the government of any problems that a corporation discovers on its own. However, the existence of a compliance program is not sufficient, in and of itself, to justify not charging a corporation for criminal misconduct undertaken by its officers, directors, employees, or agents. In addition, the nature of some crimes, e.g., antitrust violations, may be such that national law enforcement policies mandate prosecutions of corporations notwithstanding the existence of a compliance program.

    Comment: The existence of a corporate compliance program, even one that specifically prohibited the very conduct in question, does not absolve the corporation from criminal liability under the doctrine of respondeat superior. *See United States v. Basic Constr. Co.*, 711 F.2d 570, 573 (4th Cir. 1983) ("[A] corporation may be held criminally responsible for antitrust violations committed by its employees if they were acting within the scope of their authority, or apparent authority, and for the benefit of the corporation, even if . . . such acts were against corporate policy or express instructions."). As explained in *United States v. Potter*, 463 F.3d 9 (1st Cir. 2006), a corporation cannot "avoid liability by adopting abstract rules" that forbid its agents from engaging in illegal acts, because "[e]ven a specific directive to an agent or employee or honest efforts to police such rules do not automatically free the company for the wrongful acts of agents." Id. at 25–26. *See also United States v. Hilton Hotels Corp.*, 467 F.2d 1000, 1007 (9th Cir. 1972) (noting that a corporation "could not gain exculpation by issuing general instructions without undertaking to enforce those instructions by means commensurate with the obvious risks"); *United States v. Beusch*, 596 F.2d 871, 878 (9th Cir. 1979) ("[A] corporation may be liable for acts of its employees done contrary to express instructions and policies, but . . . the existence of such instructions and policies may be considered in determining whether the employee in fact acted to benefit the corporation.").

While the Department recognizes that no compliance program can ever prevent all criminal activity by a corporation's employees, the critical factors in evaluating any program are whether the program is adequately designed for maximum effectiveness in preventing and detecting wrongdoing by employees and whether corporate management is enforcing the program or is tacitly encouraging or pressuring employees to engage in misconduct to achieve business objectives. The Department has no formulaic requirements regarding corporate compliance programs. The fundamental questions any prosecutor should ask are: Is the corporation's compliance program well designed? Is the program being applied earnestly and in good faith? Does the corporation's compliance program work? In answering these questions, the prosecutor should consider the comprehensiveness of the compliance program; the extent and pervasiveness of the criminal misconduct; the number and level of the corporate employees involved; the seriousness, duration, and frequency of the misconduct; and any remedial actions taken by the corporation, including, for example, disciplinary action against past violators uncovered by the prior compliance program, and revisions to corporate compliance programs in light of lessons learned .... Prosecutors should also consider the promptness of any disclosure of wrongdoing to the government. In evaluating compliance programs, prosecutors may consider whether the corporation has established corporate governance mechanisms that can effectively detect and prevent misconduct. For example, do the corporation's directors exercise independent review over proposed corporate actions rather than unquestioningly ratifying officers' recommendations; are internal audit functions conducted at a level sufficient to ensure their independence and accuracy; and have the directors established an information and reporting system in the organization reasonably designed to provide management and directors with timely and accurate information sufficient to allow them to reach an informed decision regarding the organization's compliance with the law. *See, e.g., In re Caremark Int'l Inc. Derivative Litig.*, 698 A.2d 959, 968–70 (Del. Ch. 1996).

Prosecutors should therefore attempt to determine whether a corporation's compliance program is merely a "paper program" or whether it was designed, implemented, reviewed, and revised, as appropriate, in an effective manner. In addition, prosecutors should determine whether the corporation has provided for a staff sufficient to audit, document, analyze, and utilize the results of the corporation's compliance efforts. Prosecutors also should determine whether the corporation's employees are adequately informed about the compliance program and are convinced of the corporation's commitment to it. This will enable the prosecutor to make an informed decision as to whether the corporation has adopted and implemented a truly effective compliance program that, when consistent with other federal law enforcement policies, may result in a decision to charge only the corporation's employees and agents or to mitigate charges or sanctions against the corporation.

Compliance programs should be designed to detect the particular types of misconduct most likely to occur in a particular corporation's line of business. Many corporations operate in complex regulatory environments outside the normal experience of criminal prosecutors. Accordingly, prosecutors should consult with relevant federal and state agencies with the expertise to evaluate the adequacy of a program's design and implementation. For instance, state and federal banking, insurance, and medical boards, the Department of Defense, the Department of Health and Human Services, the Environmental Protection Agency, and the Securities and Exchange Commission have considerable experience with compliance programs and can be helpful to a prosecutor in evaluating such programs. In addition, the Fraud Section of the Criminal Division, the Commercial Litigation Branch of the Civil Division, and the Environmental Crimes Section of the Environment and Natural Resources Division can assist United States Attorneys' Offices in finding the appropriate agency office(s) for such consultation.

Appendix 3

Excerpts from the Federal Sentencing Guidelines Manual

Chapter Eight—Sentencing of Organizations

Introductory Commentary

The guidelines and policy statements in this chapter apply when the convicted defendant is an organization. Organizations can act only through agents and, under federal criminal law, generally are vicariously liable for offenses committed by their agents. At the same time, individual agents are responsible for their own criminal conduct. Federal prosecutions of organizations therefore frequently involve individual and organizational codefendants. Convicted individual agents of organizations are sentenced in accordance with the guidelines and policy statements in the preceding chapters. This chapter is designed so that the sanctions imposed upon organizations and their agents, taken together, will provide just punishment, adequate deterrence, and incentives for organizations to maintain internal mechanisms for preventing, detecting, and reporting criminal conduct.

This chapter reflects the following general principles:

First, the court must, whenever practicable, order the organization to remedy any harm caused by the offense. The resources expended to remedy the harm should not be viewed as punishment, but rather as a means of making victims whole for the harm caused.

Second, if the organization operated primarily for a criminal purpose or primarily by criminal means, the fine should be set sufficiently high to divest the organization of all its assets.

Third, the fine range for any other organization should be based on the seriousness of the offense and the culpability of the organization. The seriousness of the offense generally will be reflected by the greatest of the pecuniary gain, the pecuniary loss, or the amount in a guideline offense level fine table. Culpability generally will be determined by six factors that the sentencing court must consider. The four factors that increase the ultimate punishment of an organization are: (i) the involvement in or tolerance of criminal activity; (ii) the prior history of the organization; (iii) the violation of an order; and (iv) the obstruction of justice. The two factors that mitigate the ultimate punishment of an organization are: (i) the existence of an effective compliance and ethics program; and (ii) self-reporting, cooperation, or acceptance of responsibility.

Fourth, probation is an appropriate sentence for an organizational defendant when needed to ensure that another sanction will be fully implemented, or to ensure that steps will be taken within the organization to reduce the likelihood of future criminal conduct.

These guidelines offer incentives to organizations to reduce and ultimately eliminate criminal conduct by providing a structural foundation from which an organization may self-police its own conduct through an effective compliance and ethics program. The prevention and detection of criminal conduct, as facilitated by an effective compliance and ethics program, will assist an organization in encouraging ethical conduct and in complying fully with all applicable laws.

Part B - Remedying Harm from Criminal Conduct, and Effective Compliance and Ethics Program

1. Remedying Harm from Criminal Conduct

Introductory Commentary

As a general principle, the court should require that the organization take all appropriate steps to provide compensation to victims and otherwise remedy the harm caused or threatened by the offense. A restitution order or an order of probation requiring restitution can be used to compensate identifiable victims of the offense. A remedial order or an order of probation requiring community service can be used to reduce or eliminate the harm threatened, or to repair the harm caused by the offense, when that harm or threatened harm would otherwise not be remedied. An order of notice to victims can be used to notify unidentified victims of the offense.

* * *

2. Effective Compliance and Ethics Program

§8B2.1. Effective Compliance and Ethics Program

(a) To have an effective compliance and ethics program, for purposes of subsection (f) of §8C2.5 (Culpability Score) and subsection (c)(1) of §8D1.4 (Recommended Conditions of Probation - Organizations), an organization shall—

　　(1) exercise due diligence to prevent and detect criminal conduct; and

　　(2) otherwise promote an organizational culture that encourages ethical conduct and a commitment to compliance with the law.

　　Such compliance and ethics program shall be reasonably designed, implemented, and enforced so that the program is generally effective in preventing and detecting criminal conduct. The failure to prevent or detect the instant offense does not necessarily mean that the program is not generally effective in preventing and detecting criminal conduct.

(b) Due diligence and the promotion of an organizational culture that encourages ethical conduct and a commitment to compliance with the law within the meaning of subsection (a) minimally require the following:

(1) The organization shall establish standards and procedures to prevent and detect criminal conduct.

(2) (A) The organization's governing authority shall be knowledgeable about the content and operation of the compliance and ethics program and shall exercise reasonable oversight with respect to the implementation and effectiveness of the compliance and ethics program.

(B) High-level personnel of the organization shall ensure that the organization has an effective compliance and ethics program, as described in this guideline. Specific individual(s) within high-level personnel shall be assigned overall responsibility for the compliance and ethics program.

(C) Specific individual(s) within the organization shall be delegated day-to-day operational responsibility for the compliance and ethics program. Individual(s) with operational responsibility shall report periodically to high-level personnel and, as appropriate, to the governing authority, or an appropriate subgroup of the governing authority, on the effectiveness of the compliance and ethics program. To carry out such operational responsibility, such individual(s) shall be given adequate resources, appropriate authority, and direct access to the governing authority or an appropriate sub-group of the governing authority.

(3) The organization shall use reasonable efforts not to include within the substantial authority personnel of the organization any individual whom the organization knew, or should have known through the exercise of due diligence, has engaged in illegal activities or other conduct inconsistent with an effective compliance and ethics program.

(4) (A) The organization shall take reasonable steps to communicate periodically and in a practical manner its standards and procedures, and other aspects of the compliance and ethics program, to the individuals referred to in subparagraph (B) by conducting effective training programs and otherwise disseminating information appropriate to such individuals' respective roles and responsibilities.

(B) The individuals referred to in subparagraph (A) are the members of the governing authority, high-level personnel, substantial authority personnel, the organization's employees, and, as appropriate, the organization's agents.

(5) The organization shall take reasonable steps—

(A) to ensure that the organization's compliance and ethics program is followed, including monitoring and auditing to detect criminal conduct;

(B) to evaluate periodically the effectiveness of the organization's compliance and ethics program; and

(C) to have and publicize a system, which may include mechanisms that allow for anonymity or confidentiality, whereby the organization's employees and agents may report or seek guidance regarding potential or actual criminal conduct without fear of retaliation.

(6) The organization's compliance and ethics program shall be promoted and enforced consistently throughout the organization through (A) appropriate incentives to perform in accordance with the compliance and ethics program; and (B) appropriate disciplinary measures for engaging in criminal conduct and for failing to take reasonable steps to prevent or detect criminal conduct.

(7) After criminal conduct has been detected, the organization shall take reasonable steps to respond appropriately to the criminal conduct and to prevent further similar criminal conduct, including making any necessary modifications to the organization's compliance and ethics program.

(c) In implementing subsection (b), the organization shall periodically assess the risk of criminal conduct and shall take appropriate steps to design, implement, or modify each requirement set forth in subsection (b) to reduce the risk of criminal conduct identified through this process.

Commentary

Application Notes:

1. **Definitions**—For purposes of this guideline:

"Compliance and ethics program" means a program designed to prevent and detect criminal conduct.

"Governing authority" means the (A) the Board of Directors; or (B) if the organization does not have a Board of Directors, the highest-level governing body of the organization.

"High-level personnel of the organization" and "substantial authority personnel" have the meaning given those terms in the Commentary to §8A1.2 (Application Instructions - Organizations).

"Standards and procedures" means standards of conduct and internal controls that are reasonably capable of reducing the likelihood of criminal conduct.

2. **Factors to Consider in Meeting Requirements of this Guideline—**

   (A) **In General**—Each of the requirements set forth in this guideline shall be met by an organization; however, in determining what specific actions are necessary to meet those requirements, factors that shall be considered include: (i) applicable industry practice or the standards called for by any applicable governmental regulation; (ii) the size of the organization; and (iii) similar misconduct.

   (B) **Applicable Governmental Regulation and Industry Practice**—An organization's failure to incorporate and follow applicable industry practice or the standards called for by any applicable governmental regulation weighs against a finding of an effective compliance and ethics program.

   (C) **The Size of the Organization—**

      (i) **In General**—The formality and scope of actions that an organization shall take to meet the requirements of this guideline, including the necessary features of the organization's standards and procedures, depend on the size of the organization.

      (ii) **Large Organizations**—A large organization generally shall devote more formal operations and greater resources in meeting the requirements of this guideline than shall a small organization. As appropriate, a large organization should encourage small organizations (especially those that have, or seek to have, a business relationship with the large organization) to implement effective compliance and ethics programs.

(iii) **Small Organizations**—In meeting the requirements of this guideline, small organizations shall demonstrate the same degree of commitment to ethical conduct and compliance with the law as large organizations. However, a small organization may meet the requirements of this guideline with less formality and fewer resources than would be expected of large organizations. In appropriate circumstances, reliance on existing resources and simple systems can demonstrate a degree of commitment that, for a large organization, would only be demonstrated through more formally planned and implemented systems.

Examples of the informality and use of fewer resources with which a small organization may meet the requirements of this guideline include the following: (I) the governing authority's discharge of its responsibility for oversight of the compliance and ethics program by directly managing the organization's compliance and ethics efforts; (II) training employees through informal staff meetings, and monitoring through regular "walk-arounds" or continuous observation while managing the organization; (III) using available personnel, rather than employing separate staff, to carry out the compliance and ethics program; and (IV) modeling its own compliance and ethics program on existing, well-regarded compliance and ethics programs and best practices of other similar organizations.

(D) **Recurrence of Similar Misconduct**—Recurrence of similar misconduct creates doubt regarding whether the organization took reasonable steps to meet the requirements of this guideline. For purposes of this sub-paragraph, "similar misconduct" has the meaning given that term in the Commentary to §8A1.2 (Application Instructions - Organizations).

3. **Application of Subsection (b)(2)**—High-level personnel and substantial authority personnel of the organization shall be knowledgeable about the content and operation of the compliance and ethics program, shall perform their assigned duties consistent with the exercise of due diligence, and shall promote an organizational culture that encourages ethical conduct and a commitment to compliance with the law.

If the specific individual(s) assigned overall responsibility for the compliance and ethics program does not have day-to-day operational responsibility for the program, then the individual(s) with day-to-day operational responsibility for the program typically should, no less than annually, give the governing authority or an appropriate subgroup thereof information on the implementation and effectiveness of the compliance and ethics program.

4. **Application of Subsection (b)(3)**—

(A) **Consistency with Other Law**—Nothing in subsection (b)(3) is intended to require conduct inconsistent with any Federal, State, or local law, including any law governing employment or hiring practices.

(B) **Implementation**—In implementing subsection (b)(3), the organization shall hire and promote individuals so as to ensure that all individuals within the high-level personnel and substantial authority personnel of the organization will perform their assigned duties in a manner consistent with the exercise of due diligence and the promotion of an organizational culture that encourages ethical conduct and a commitment to compliance with the law under subsection (a). With respect to the hiring or promotion of such individuals, an organization shall consider the relatedness of the individual's illegal activities and other misconduct (i.e., other conduct inconsistent with an effective compliance and ethics program) to the specific responsibilities the individual is anticipated to be assigned and other factors such as: (i) the recency of the individual's illegal activities and other misconduct; and (ii) whether the individual has engaged in other such illegal activities and other such misconduct.

5. **Application of Subsection (b)(6)**—Adequate discipline of individuals responsible for an offense is a necessary component of enforcement; however, the form of discipline that will be appropriate will be case specific.

6. **Application of Subsection (b)(7)**— Subsection (b)(7) has two aspects.

First, the organization should respond appropriately to the criminal conduct. The organization should take reasonable steps, as warranted under the circumstances, to remedy the harm resulting from the criminal conduct. These steps may include, where appropriate, providing restitution to identifiable victims, as well as other forms of remediation. Other reasonable steps to respond appropriately to the criminal conduct may include self-reporting and cooperation with authorities.

Second, the organization should act appropriately to prevent further similar criminal conduct, including assessing the compliance and ethics program and making modifications necessary to ensure the program is effective. The steps taken should be consistent with subsections (b)(5) and (c) and may include the use of an outside professional advisor to ensure adequate assessment and implementation of any modifications.

7. **Application of Subsection (c)**—To meet the requirements of subsection (c), an organization shall:

   (A) Assess periodically the risk that criminal conduct will occur, including assessing the following:

   (i) The nature and seriousness of such criminal conduct.

   (ii) The likelihood that certain criminal conduct may occur because of the nature of the organization's business. If, because of the nature of an organization's business, there is a substantial risk that certain types of criminal conduct may occur, the organization shall take reasonable steps to prevent and detect that type of criminal conduct. For example, an organization that, due to the nature of its business, employs sales personnel who have flexibility to set prices shall establish standards and procedures designed to prevent and detect price-fixing. An organization that, due to the nature of its business, employs sales personnel who have flexibility to represent the material characteristics of a product shall establish standards and procedures designed to prevent and detect fraud.

   (iii) The prior history of the organization. The prior history of an organization may indicate types of criminal conduct that it shall take actions to prevent and detect.

(B) Prioritize periodically, as appropriate, the actions taken pursuant to any requirement set forth in subsection (b), in order to focus on preventing and detecting the criminal conduct identified under subparagraph (A) of this note as most serious, and most likely, to occur.

(C) Modify, as appropriate, the actions taken pursuant to any requirement set forth in subsection (b) to reduce the risk of criminal conduct identified under subparagraph (A) of this note as most serious, and most likely, to occur.

Commentary

Background: This section sets forth the requirements for an effective compliance and ethics program. This section responds to section 805(a)(2)(5) of the Sarbanes-Oxley Act of 2002, Public Law 107–204, which directed the Commission to review and amend, as appropriate, the guidelines and related policy statements to ensure that the guidelines that apply to organizations in this chapter "are sufficient to deter and punish organizational criminal misconduct."

The requirements set forth in this guideline are intended to achieve reasonable prevention and detection of criminal conduct for which the organization would be vicariously liable. The prior diligence of an organization in seeking to prevent and detect criminal conduct has a direct bearing on the appropriate penalties and probation terms for the organization if it is convicted and sentenced for a criminal offense.

PART C—FINES
1. Determining the Fine—Criminal Purpose Organizations

§8C1.1. Determining the Fine—Criminal Purpose Organizations

If, upon consideration of the nature and circumstances of the offense and the history and characteristics of the organization, the court determines that the organization operated primarily for a criminal purpose or primarily by criminal means, the fine shall be set at an amount (subject to the statutory maximum) sufficient to divest the organization of all its net assets. When this section applies, Subpart 2 (Determining the Fine - Other Organizations) and §8C3.4 (Fines Paid by Owners of Closely Held Organizations) do not apply.

Commentary

Application Note:

1. "Net assets," as used in this section, means the assets remaining after payment of all legitimate claims against assets by known innocent bona fide creditors.

Background: This guideline addresses the case in which the court, based upon an examination of the nature and circumstances of the offense and the history and characteristics of the organization, determines that the organization was operated primarily for a criminal purpose (e.g., a front for a scheme that was designed to commit fraud; an organization established to participate in the illegal manufacture, importation, or distribution of a controlled substance) or operated primarily by criminal means (e.g., a hazardous waste disposal business that had no legitimate means of disposing of hazardous waste). In such a case, the fine shall be set at an amount sufficient to remove all of the organization's net assets. If the extent of the assets of the organization is unknown, the maximum fine authorized by statute should be imposed, absent innocent bona fide creditors.

* * *

§8C2.5. Culpability Score

(a) Start with 5 points and apply subsections (b) through (g) below.

* * *

(f) Effective Compliance and Ethics Program

(1) If the offense occurred even though the organization had in place at the time of the offense an effective compliance and ethics program, as provided in §8B2.1 (Effective Compliance and Ethics Program), subtract 3 points.

(2) Subsection (f)(1) shall not apply if, after becoming aware of an offense, the organization unreasonably delayed reporting the offense to appropriate governmental authorities.

(3) (A) Except as provided in subparagraphs (B) and (C), subsection (f)(1) shall not apply if an individual within high-level personnel of the organization, a person within high-level personnel of the unit of the organization within which the offense was committed where the unit had 200 or more employees, or an individual described in §8B2.1(b)(2)(B) or (C), participated in, condoned, or was willfully ignorant of the offense.

(B) There is a rebuttable presumption, for purposes of subsection (f)(1), that the organization did not have an effective compliance and ethics program if an individual—

(i) within high-level personnel of a small organization; or

> > (ii) within substantial authority personnel, but not within high-level personnel, of any organization, participated in, condoned, or was willfully ignorant of, the offense.
> (C) Subparagraphs (A) and (B) shall not apply if—
> > (i) the individual or individuals with operational responsibility for the compliance and ethics program (see §8B2.1(b)(2)(C)) have direct reporting obligations to the governing authority or an appropriate subgroup thereof (e.g., an audit committee of the board of directors);
> > (ii) the compliance and ethics program detected the offense before discovery outside the organization or before such discovery was reasonably likely;
> > (iii) the organization promptly reported the offense to appropriate governmental authorities; and
> > (iv) no individual with operational responsibility for the compliance and ethics program participated in, condoned, or was willfully ignorant of the offense.

(g) Self-Reporting, Cooperation, and Acceptance of Responsibility

If more than one applies, use the greatest:

(1) If the organization (A) prior to an imminent threat of disclosure or government investigation; and (B) within a reasonably prompt time after becoming aware of the offense, reported the offense to appropriate governmental authorities, fully cooperated in the investigation, and clearly demonstrated recognition and affirmative acceptance of responsibility for its criminal conduct, subtract 5 points; or

(2) If the organization fully cooperated in the investigation and clearly demonstrated recognition and affirmative acceptance of responsibility for its criminal conduct, subtract 2 points; or

(3) If the organization clearly demonstrated recognition and affirmative acceptance of responsibility for its criminal conduct, subtract 1 point.

Commentary

Application Notes:

1. Definitions.—For purposes of this guideline, "condoned", "prior criminal adjudication," "similar misconduct," "substantial authority personnel," and "willfully ignorant of the offense" have the meaning given those terms in Application Note 3 of the Commentary to §8A1.2 (Application Instructions - Organizations).

   "Small Organization", for purposes of subsection (f)(3), means an organization that, at the time of the instant offense, had fewer than 200 employees.

   * * *

3. "High-level personnel of the organization" is defined in the Commentary to §8A1.2 (Application Instructions - Organizations). With respect to a unit with 200 or more employees, "high-level personnel of a unit of the organization" means agents within the unit who set the policy for or control that unit. For example, if the managing agent of a unit with 200 employees participated in an offense, three points would be added under subsection (b)(3); if that organization had 1,000 employees and the managing agent of the unit with 200 employees were also within high-level personnel of the organization in its entirety, four

points (rather than three) would be added under subsection (b)(2).

* * *

10. Subsection (f)(2) contemplates that the organization will be allowed a reasonable period of time to conduct an internal investigation. In addition, no reporting is required by subsection (f)(2) or (f)(3)(C)(iii) if the organization reasonably concluded, based on the information then available, that no offense had been committed.

12. "Appropriate governmental authorities," as used in subsections (f) and (g)(1), means the federal or state law enforcement, regulatory, or program officials having jurisdiction over such matter. To qualify for a reduction under subsection (g)(1), the report to appropriate governmental authorities must be made under the direction of the organization.

11. For purposes of subsection (f)(3)(C)(i), an individual has "direct reporting obligations" to the governing authority or an appropriate subgroup thereof if the individual has express authority to communicate personally to the governing authority or appropriate subgroup thereof (A) promptly on any matter involving criminal conduct or potential criminal conduct, and (B) no less than annually on the implementation and effectiveness of the compliance and ethics program."

13. To qualify for a reduction under subsection (g)(1) or (g)(2), cooperation must be both timely and thorough. To be timely, the cooperation must begin essentially at the same time as the organization is officially notified of a criminal investigation. To be thorough, the cooperation should include the disclosure of all pertinent information known by the organization. A prime test of whether the organization has disclosed all pertinent information is whether

the information is sufficient for law enforcement personnel to identify the nature and extent of the offense and the individual(s) responsible for the criminal conduct. However, the cooperation to be measured is the cooperation of the organization itself, not the cooperation of individuals within the organization. If, because of the lack of cooperation of particular individual(s), neither the organization nor law enforcement personnel are able to identify the culpable individual(s) within the organization despite the organization's efforts to cooperate fully, the organization may still be given credit for full cooperation.

14. Entry of a plea of guilty prior to the commencement of trial combined with truthful admission of involvement in the offense and related conduct ordinarily will constitute significant evidence of affirmative acceptance of responsibility under subsection (g), unless outweighed by conduct of the organization that is inconsistent with such acceptance of responsibility. This adjustment is not intended to apply to an organization that puts the government to its burden of proof at trial by denying the essential factual elements of guilt, is convicted, and only then admits guilt and expresses remorse. Conviction by trial, however, does not automatically preclude an organization from consideration for such a reduction. In rare situations, an organization may clearly demonstrate an acceptance of responsibility for its criminal conduct even though it exercises its constitutional right to a trial. This may occur, for example, where an organization goes to trial to assert and preserve issues that do not relate to factual guilt (e.g., to make a constitutional challenge to a statute or a challenge to the applicability of a statute to its conduct). In each such instance, however, a determination that an organization has accepted responsibility will be based primarily upon pretrial statements and conduct.

15. In making a determination with respect to subsection (g), the court may determine that the chief executive officer or highest ranking employee of an organization should appear at sentencing in order to signify that the organization has clearly demonstrated recognition and affirmative acceptance of responsibility.

* * *

Part D—Organizational Probation

Introductory Commentary

Section 8D1.1 sets forth the circumstances under which a sentence to a term of probation is required. Sections 8D1.2 through 8D1.4, and 8F1.1, address the length of the probation term, conditions of probation, and violations of probation conditions.

* * *

§8D1.4. Recommended Conditions of Probation— Organizations (Policy Statement)

(a) The court may order the organization, at its expense and in the format and media specified by the court, to publicize the nature of the offense committed, the fact of conviction, the nature of the punishment imposed, and the steps that will be taken to prevent the recurrence of similar offenses.

(b) If probation is imposed under §8D1.1, the following conditions may be appropriate:

   (1) The organization shall develop and submit to the court an effective compliance and ethics program consistent with §8B2.1 (Effective Compliance and Ethics Program). The organization shall include in its submission a schedule for implementation of the compliance and ethics program.

(2) Upon approval by the court of a program referred to in paragraph (1), the organization shall notify its employees and shareholders of its criminal behavior and its program referred to in paragraph (1). Such notice shall be in a form prescribed by the court.

(3) The organization shall make periodic submissions to the court or probation officer, at intervals specified by the court, (A) reporting on the organization's financial condition and results of business operations, and accounting for the disposition of all funds received, and (B) reporting on the organization's progress in implementing the program referred to in paragraph (1). Among other things, reports under subparagraph (B) shall disclose any criminal prosecution, civil litigation, or administrative proceeding commenced against the organization, or any investigation or formal inquiry by governmental authorities of which the organization learned since its last report.

(4) The organization shall notify the court or probation officer immediately upon learning of (A) any material adverse change in its business or financial condition or prospects, or (B) the commencement of any bankruptcy proceeding, major civil litigation, criminal prosecution, or administration proceeding against the organization, or any investigation or formal inquiry by governmental authorities regarding the organization.

(5) The organization shall submit to: (A) a reasonable number of regular or unannounced examinations of its books and records at appropriate business premises by the probation officer or experts engaged by the court; and (B) interrogation of knowledgeable individuals within the organization. Compensation to and costs of any experts engaged by the court shall be paid by the organization.

(6) The organization shall make periodic payments, as specified by the court, in the following priority: (A) restitution; (B) fine; and (C) any other monetary sanction.

Commentary

Application Note:

1. In determining the conditions to be imposed when probation is ordered under §8D1.1, the court should consider the views of any governmental regulatory body that oversees conduct of the organization relating to the instant offense. To assess the efficacy of a compliance and ethics program submitted by the organization, the court may employ appropriate experts who shall be afforded access to all material possessed by the organization that is necessary for a comprehensive assessment of the proposed program. The court should approve any program that appears reasonably calculated to prevent and detect criminal conduct, as long as it is consistent with §8B2.1 (Effective Compliance and Ethics Program), and any applicable statutory and regulatory requirements.

   Periodic reports submitted in accordance with subsection (b)(3) should be provided to any governmental regulatory body that oversees conduct of the organization relating to the instant offense.

About the Author

Aaron Murphy is a partner with a major international law firm. In the course of handling bribery investigations on five continents, he has been held at gunpoint by the Indonesian military, detained by Kazakhstan customs officers, informed of how cheap it is to have acid thrown in someone's face, and warned of how simple it is to "make someone go away." Throughout, he has been informed countless times that he "just doesn't understand how business is done here."

Index